Ain't Misbehavin'

Laverne Antrobus

PRENTICE HALL LIFE

If life is what you make it, then making it better starts here.

What we learn today can change our lives tomorrow. It can change our goals or change our minds; open up new opportunities or simply inspire us to make a difference. That's why we have created a new breed of books that do more to help you make more of your life.

Whether you want more confidence or less stress, a new skill or a different perspective, we've designed *Prentice Hall Life* books to help you to make a change for the better. Together with our authors we share a commitment to bring you the brightest ideas and best ways to manage your life, work and wealth.

In these pages we hope you'll find the ideas you need for the life *you* want. Go on, help yourself.

It's what you make it

Ain't Misbehavin'

How to understand your child's behaviour
and get the best from them

Laverne Antrobus

PEARSON
Prentice Hall
LIFE

Pearson Education Limited
Edinburgh Gate
Harlow
Essex CM20 2JE
England

ISBN 978-0-273-71266-4

Commissioning Editor: Emma Shackleton
Project Editor: Helena Caldon
Designer: Annette Peppis
Cover Design: R&D&Co
Senior Production Controller: Man Fai Lau

Printed and bound by Henry Ling, UK

The Publisher's policy is to use paper manufactured from sustainable forests.

Essex County
Council Libraries

Contents

What should I expect?

It is quite right that parents should have high expectations of their children's behaviour; we are all delighted when we are complimented on how well our child behaves – and, of course, there is nothing quite as awful as when the opposite happens and we are embarrassed by his antics. However, often when people have children they bring to their parenting definite ideas about how they want their child to behave; so when they find that he is not reading the same script as them, they feel completely and utterly lost.

As we all know, the way in which we respond to each of our children can be a completely different, and often unpredictable, experience. I want you to remember this as you read on because I strongly believe that having this knowledge can give you as a parent the space to feel you can get things both right and wrong. It can also help you to learn how to handle situations differently the next time.

In the following chapters I will try to guide you through the maze of misbehaviour and equip you with the skills you need in order to communicate better with your child and improve his behaviour, while at the same time strengthening (rather than damaging) your relationship with him.

Every parent needs to feel that they are doing a good job in bringing up their children because at times parenting can feel like a thankless task. So I hope this book can offer you at least some of the help, advice and, most importantly, support that you need to address these issues and create a happy and harmonious family life.

How we develop parenting skills

We tend to form our ideas about how our children should behave primarily from how our parents brought us up and how we behaved. We also have numerous opportunities to see what is acceptable to us (and others), and what is not, when we are out socializing with other families or with relatives. Watching and observing how other parents manage their children is a good way to pick up the dos and don'ts of parenting, and may also help you to think about which approach might work for you in your situation.

Behaviour starts at home

All children develop individually and at different rates, and as a parent you will inevitably experience ups and downs in your own levels of confidence and efforts to cope with their behaviour as it changes.

Often when I sit with families, parents present their view of how their child relates to them: they tell me that she is distant or defiant, or that they are worried about her general behaviour and the impact it is having on her and her family.

My job is to listen and to observe the family in action and to learn as much as I can about them as a unit. Once I have this knowledge I can then help the family make sense of where her behaviours may have come from, using both their narrative accounts and the information I have from seeing them all together.

This is often the key to resolving behaviour issues: identify the problems within the family, or around it, and see what is affecting a child. If you can learn how to deal with situations without anger, resentment or feeling like you want to give up, and instead choose to approach issues with love, interest and a commitment to improving the situation; you can shape and change your child's behaviour for the better.

It is not always easy to listen to someone's observations on how your family situation is being managed, but an outsider's perspective is invaluable if you can take it on board without being defensive. It can be tricky to really see what is before your very eyes when you are in the throes of family life; the pace at which many of us conduct our lives does not allow for the sort of reflective space we need to be able to monitor how

Watch yourself!

Think about how you behave in different social settings and how you change and adapt your behaviour depending on the situation. There are not many of us who, hand on heart, could say that we behave in the same way with everyone we meet. Think about your own behaviour, then watch your children and you will notice all the subtle adaptations that each individual in your family makes in different settings.

we are managing as a family. By developing your skills of self-reflection and by asking questions of yourself, or of trusted others around you, about how some of your behaviours may be impacting on your child's behaviour, you will be giving yourself, and the immense role that you are taking on, the justice that it deserves.

Your child learns from you: she will watch you in order to learn how to behave and you will also probably have told her how you expect her to behave. I suspect that there have also been times when you have heard her using the same words that you use, or even seen her trying to get others to behave in the way that she wants them to. This is evidence of the powerful relationship that you have with your child.

Having read that your behaviour is key, I wonder how many of you are saying, 'Oh, great, if the good stuff is down to me then the bad stuff must be my mess as well.' But it's really not that simple. I believe that there are aspects of your child's behaviour that are directly attributable to you, but there are also aspects that belong to the individual. Our job as a parent is to help our children bring their own unique characters and personalities to the table so that we can then show them which are the bits that work and which are the bits that might get them into a bit of bother.

For example, if you are a loud person who uses this style of communication to get your point across then you will be giving your child permission to communicate in this way. When it is pointed out to parents that this is how their children are behaving, often these same parents, as a defence, will say that their children do not behave badly at home.

So think carefully about how you use your voice: if you have a habit of shouting, consider its impact on everyone around you. It really isn't helpful to them, even if it does mean that you get things done.

You will probably find that, with children, it is often more effective to speak to them using an ordinary tone of voice and, when you feel that you need to put your point of view across more forcefully, to use language rather than tone to make your point. It can also be more powerful if you express yourself in statements beginning with 'I'.

Remember, the clearer you are the easier it will be for your child to get the message. And, most of all, don't fall into the trap of always expecting her to understand exactly what it is you want her to do.

For parents, part of establishing good communication with your child is being a model for the behaviour you want to see in her. In this case this will involve characteristics such as listening, complying with reasonable requests, staying calm in difficult or emotional situations and communicating clearly. It is also important for you to acknowledge when you have done something well, or if something has gone wrong.

So in theory you want your behaviour to be exemplary and able to demonstrate to your children that you have a (mostly) balanced attitude and approach to life and that you can deal calmly with most things that it throws at you.

No sexual stereotyping, please!

Whether you have a son or a daughter, try to be aware of the impact of your response in relation to your child's sex. It's amazing how easy it is to miss these more subtle reactions: for example, games with boys are often described as being more rough and tough. In this way the language that adults use to describe boys or girls will give your child information about how his parents expect him to behave. Some of this can happen fairly unconsciously, as many of us have been carefully programmed to speak in definitive terms about different genders, but this makes it even more important for us to pay attention to the message we are sending.

It might seem obvious to say that gender stereotyping is not helpful, but it happens; so I would urge all parents to reflect carefully on what they are saying to their child. Are you boxing him into a way of behaving that is right for you but not right for him?

Children will naturally find a way of playing and developing that reflects their character, and what each child needs in order to develop is support. If you try to impose defining expectations on your child you will only limit his development.

If you can't see the truth of this, just think back to your own childhood and how your own parents or close family members described you in terms of gender. I bet many of you can recall how it made you feel when you heard people comment on your behaviour by saying things such as, 'She's a real girl/boy isn't she?'

What parents can expect

Having said all of that, let's be clear about what parents should realistically expect from their children. Parents like to feel, and should to a certain extent be, in control of their children; but control on its own is a recipe for disaster. Control should always be carefully balanced with care. This includes love, affection and warmth, and without this balance the rewards of parenting for you will be few – not to mention how uncomfortable it will feel for your child!

As your child develops and grows, his capacity for negotiation will also begin to develop. As parents you need to be on hand to respond to this change by helping him to assert his growing independence, and by respecting this while still maintaining the balance of control in your relationship with him. A good way of doing this is to listen to your child and show him that thinking about and addressing potential sticking points together is a good way to solve problems.

As a parent I believe it is reasonable to expect that your child will be able to:

- Demonstrate affection.
- Listen to and follow your instructions.
- Show you that he is upset.
- Express his frustration in a variety of ways.

In order to achieve this situation with your child, you need to establish good communication with him.

Your relationship with your child starts at birth...

A baby's cry can signal distress, hunger or just that she's fed up and in need of some attention. And here is something you need to recognize: communication at this stage of a baby's development is at a basic level. Babies have to communicate their needs to their parents in order to survive and to ensure they are looked after properly. Thus how we learn to respond to our child in these early months sows the seeds of our later relationship with her: i.e. whether we continue to listen and think about her physical and emotional needs.

A phrase that you may have heard, and one which is particularly helpful, is the idea of babies and young children needing to feel that they are being held in the mind of their parents. This essentially means that a child needs to feel that the significant adult taking care of her is someone who thinks about her and considers her general wellbeing at all times.

This is a part of parenting that never stops. I believe many parents quite naturally hold their children in mind and this leads to them being able to separate from their children in a good way – because their children feel secure even when their parents are not physically present. For example, when a young child is first left at a playgroup or with an alternative caregiver, the way in which she copes with and behaves in this unfamiliar situation is very much determined by how secure she feels in her parents' care.

Start as you mean to go on

So how can you develop a style of parenting that will lead to a successful holding in mind and your child feeling emotionally secure? Think back to how you felt after you had your baby, or babies. Some parents (but particularly mothers) feel physically on the mend and emotionally able to cope quite soon after the arrival of their baby, but this is not always the case.

Recalling this phase of your recovery and behaviour will help you to notice how your own behaviour affected that of your baby. If you felt particularly tired, the demands your baby placed on you probably felt greater, which might have meant that you felt even more tired and so you were perhaps less predictable in your contact. Similarly, if you felt nervous he will most definitely have picked up on this.

What inevitably happens during these early days, or months, of being a parent is that the baby begins to shape his behaviour in order to elicit the responses he needs from you as his parent. Essentially this means that a baby will learn to behave in a way that he knows will provoke you to respond to him appropriately, and as your child does this he is developing his own unique template for his behaviour.

Being responsive to your child is key; children like to feel noticed and thought about. A child who feels that his parent is interested in him will experience a level of security that feels comforting. However, when a child does not feel thought about, or if he is not acknowledged, it can leave him feeling really worried about where and how he fits into the world. This in turn can lead to him needing to develop ways of behaving that will attract attention – such as through naughty behaviour. A child will often resort to this tactic to force his parents or other adults to notice him.

So right from the start, try to show your child that you appreciate him:

- Celebrate his achievements, however big or small, and don't just brush them off.
- Use praise to let him know how impressed you are with his efforts and don't complain about what is clearly his best effort, even if it falls short of your mark.
- Reinforce your verbal congratulations with physical shows of affection, but don't use physical affection only as a reward – hugs and kisses should be readily available unconditionally.
- Tell relatives about achievements and ask them to congratulate your child.
- Use stickers and treats to reward good behaviour.
- Spend special time together, DO NOT just spend money – it is not a good substitute.
- Don't compare your children to other peoples'.
- Be clear in your expectations: a two-year-old will not be able to tidy his bedroom to the standard that you can.

Parenting is about sticking in there for the long haul. If you had a tricky time at the beginning and all the feelings that you were 'supposed' to have did not come naturally to you, don't worry – there is plenty of time to make up for this. Whatever you do, don't beat yourself up for not getting it all right straight away. Remember, bringing up children is a learning curve and the key feature of successful parenting is to balance love and affection with security and control.

Your child's changing times

So children develop at different rates and in very different ways. How many times have you heard other parents say, 'Oh, we're past that stage, now she's doing…'? Parents can feel that much hangs on various developmental stages, but in fact these are just general markers and don't define all development. The key is to deal with each new stage as it occurs and not to rush the process – support and help your child to consolidate each phase.

If your child does not develop at exactly the time specified by books or knowing friends, remember this is not the end of the world. Don't panic and push her to reach that milestone, as this might just lead to her not having the opportunity she needs to get to grips with what is happening to her at a certain stage.

Every stage acts as a signpost to let us know what is ahead, and how each child passes through those stages is unique to her. It amazes me that parents feel they can be so decisive about when they have arrived at these stages and when they have gone past them. The process is not so clear cut, and one step forward, three steps back is more often how it feels.

So when thinking about some of the behavioural stages that children generally pass through it is important to focus on the emotional stages in their development too. By thinking carefully about your child's emotional development you will cultivate your own understanding of how she is processing what is happening to her.

If a child is not emotionally ready it will be difficult for her to make sense of new experiences. For example, parents often say that their child does not seem to understand how upset they are when she doesn't do the right thing. This usually happens because a child doesn't have the emotional capacity to think about another person's feelings – she is still trying to work out her own response.

As children grow they are in the throes of developing their personalities. You have probably said to family and friends that your child's personality has not really changed very much since she was very small, and that you could see what sort of person she would be from an early age. I would agree that a child's personality (in very general terms) is apparent quite early on. Parents might say their child is a really happy baby, or that she has a sweet personality or, conversely, that she is a real fighter.

You will notice all these characteristics in her, to varying degrees, as she develops. In my experience an equal number of parents pigeon-hole their child as a happy, easy baby or one that was always a bit demanding and difficult to settle. As a parent you want to nurture the whole development of your child so that she can get the balance right and be able to express discomfort, but also satisfaction when her demands are responded to appropriately.

Although every child has a unique personality, a child's behaviour usually follows a fairly predictable pattern. In

Typical behaviours

12–18 months

Starts to show resistant behaviour; this may be observed in situations where you want them to eat, take a nap or have a bath. Often around this age your child will start to have tantrums.

2 years

Appears to have two personalities: compliant/resistant and calm/aggressive. Tantrums develop and might feature crying, lashing out or biting.

3 years

Displays less frustration and anger, because as they develop their speech and language skills children begin to use them as an alternative way of communicating their frustration.

the table below I set out some of the main developmental stages, starting with a child aged one. As parents often tell me, 'Everything seemed fine until she started to walk,' and given that most babies start to walk at around one year, this seems a good place to start.

4 years

Still shows signs of difficult/stubborn behaviour. Children are now taking in a huge amount of information which they can sometimes find difficult to process, and this is their way of letting you know that they are struggling.

5 years

Able to express anger and frustration verbally and are often beginning to feel more self-assured and confident.

6–8 years

Continued testiness that aims to examine the limits that parents put in place, although children may also begin to seem a little more reasonable.

9– 12 years

Children are more able to plan ahead and also to cope with upset and disappointment.

Many of these developmental stages are completely normal and are to be expected, so think very carefully before you believe you have the worst child in the world, or that you are the worst parent in the world. Of course it can feel like everything is against you at times, but remember that your child is destined to (and will!) move through these stages. Your job is to guide her through as skilfully, calmly and considerately as you can in order to help her come out the other side.

So:

- Be patient and know that each phase will pass.
- Help your child to notice that she is behaving differently and to be able to identify when she is doing this.
- Stop and think carefully before becoming very cross: your child may not yet have the ability to be completely in control, e.g. she will have tantrums until she has developed better language skills.

In each chapter I will demonstrate how these developmental stages and ages of a child influence specific behaviours and problems. A child's ability to know right from wrong, to test boundaries, etc, will change and develop as she explores, learns and grows up. This is only natural, but her maturity (or not) will determine to a degree how you should respond – bearing in mind what she knows and understands at each given age.

Lots of parents say that their children haven't got to the next stage yet (usually when their child is showing difficult behaviour). This is often a defence mechanism for the parent and the way in which they feel they can justify how their child is behaving.

For example, take sharing. Very young children (up to the age of about three) will find sharing difficult. However, although sharing should be encouraged from an early age, be warned, too, that forcing a child to share can make her feel resentful – especially if she does not have the capacity to understand the concept. As a child gets older and realizes that toys will be returned and that she enjoys the feeling of making someone else happy, then she will naturally feel more able to share.

At about seven or eight years old, a child often begins to appreciate that another person can feel upset and she may take advantage of this knowledge and refuse to share just so she can see the upset it causes. If this happens, you need to reinforce the positive benefits of sharing and explain to her that deliberately upsetting someone isn't nice.

How does your child handle 'life'?

The normal developmental stages of children, which are part of their growth and development, do not happen in isolation. A child can be deeply affected by both ordinary and extra-ordinary life events: some, of course, cannot be predicted and this will add to the often complex changes that you will observe in his behaviour.

Many of us could create our own personal list of life events that have had, or are currently having, a negative impact on us and our children's behaviour. I want to emphasize here and now that if there has been an event that has had an impact on you as an adult it will undoubtedly have had an impact on your child. Parents often tell me that their children 'don't know' what has been happening, or that they 'haven't got a clue' or are simply 'not bothered' about the current preoccupations and struggles of their family. This is most likely not the case, though; of course children know.

It is difficult to pinpoint an actual age at which this awareness happens, but certainly I have met with parents who believe their babies began to be less settled at a certain point, and that from the age of about two years – just as they were beginning to better understand language – their child seemed to pick up on subtle changes in communication. This latter awareness will have an impact on him: either that he feels he has to be quieter, or that he needs to behave in a certain way to get more attention. However, some parents may prefer to take the view that their child is innocent and oblivious to all that is going on around him, and use this as a way of protecting themselves against the pain of knowing that their child is struggling.

But the truth is that children are fantastically wired and they will pick up on every aspect of change. In fact, many children will suffer from the added pressure of pretending that they do not know what is happening, which they take on as a way of looking after us parents. But there is only so much covering up that a child can do, and when he can no longer keep up this act then the emotions that he has been suppressing will emerge – usually in the form of difficult or defiant behaviour.

Prepare your child for change

As children are individuals they will approach and deal with situations in a variety of ways. Many children need enormous amounts of preparation to help them get ready for change but, unfortunately, life is not always that predictable. However, if there is a chance to prepare them for a change – such as moving house, the arrival of a new sibling, a separation or divorce – then you should make every effort to do so. By not doing this, and by brushing it under the carpet to deal with later, you are backing away from your job as a parent to support and manage difficulties as they arise in the best way you can.

So try to recognize this behaviour in yourself and see if you can step back from what is happening in front of you. Take the example of bringing home a new baby, and think about the massive preparations people make for this and other life-changing events.

It seems to me that people are very generous in acknowledging how difficult it is to change job, but they see having a baby as a natural event that everyone should just take in their stride. The vulnerability of a new baby can put even the most robust individuals under a lot of pressure, and it is perfectly reasonable to expect a period of shock to take over – particularly in the early days.

The reality is that life has its ups and downs, and at times this will test the resolve of parents and children alike. However, by identifying a few of the most common life-changing events we can begin to think about the possible impact on children and, of course, parents and how we might deal with these situations as, or even sometimes before, they arise.

Bringing baby home

When a new baby arrives and joins the family even well-prepared children can struggle to handle such a huge change. Parents can struggle too, and this is my point: if it is a struggle for you it is probably also a struggle for your child.

So, when you have got used to the idea of having another baby, start talking to your child about her new sibling. Allow her space to feel worried or anxious, and don't try to brush these feelings aside as if they are not real. Acknowledge that things might feel a bit strange for a while but that she will get used to it.

Spend time thinking about and preparing for the new baby – visual preparations will make the situation feel more real. Talk to your partner and child about the very real changes that are going to take place, for example, feeding, and the amount of time you will need to spend with the baby. But explain to your child that there will be special times when you can be together, too, such as when the baby is asleep and at bedtime.

Once the baby is born, plan the first 'meeting' with their sibling – perhaps with a gift, a photo or a picture – and present this to the new baby. When visitors come to see the new arrival, ask them not to forget your other child and rush immediately to the baby. Suggest that they spend time with her first so that she still feels an important part of the family.

Children may typically respond to the arrival of a new member of the family with feelings of envy and jealousy towards the baby as well as frustration and sadness at the loss of their parents' attention. All of these emotions will have associated behaviours: some will be visible, such as hitting out, while others will be less obvious, such as your child becoming withdrawn. Siblings may also demonstrate their feelings by ignoring the baby, calling her names or even trying to hurt her.

These reactions can and will change; you just need to be patient and recognize that this behaviour is an expression of the difficulty your child is having in managing this new situation. She needs to know that you can cope with her worries and that the situation will not end in disaster.

There are a few approaches that you can try which will help calm troubled waters when the baby has arrived home:

- Let your child know that you can see how hard she is finding having a new baby in the family.
- Get her involved in the care of her new sibling (for example, fetching equipment, keeping an eye on the baby). This will help her feel she can make space for the new baby.

○ Set clear rules to ensure that everybody remains safe and that your child understands how he or she is expected to behave around and towards the baby. For example, stress that running around near the baby is unsafe; be clear that picking up the baby is something that should only happen when mummy or daddy is present; and talk about how delicate her sister is, so any touching should be done very gently.

Parents separating/divorcing

Children will always be aware of difficulties in their parents' relationship. Young babies will experience it in the immediate sense, where parents are upset or preoccupied, but this memory will fade as they get older; children from about four years old will have a patchy memory of parents being together.

Regardless of age, though, the way in which you separate when a relationship has broken down will have an impact on a child. Most parents will want to separate in the least upsetting way, but often this can be very difficult when emotions are running high. Parents have to remember that children cannot understand why parents can't work things out because they have been brought up by parents to believe that most situations can be resolved happily. And so they will inevitably be distressed to see that sometimes the resolution of a situation can leave individuals feeling unhappy.

The main rules here are to:

○ Tell your child that you are separating because you feel that you cannot live together any more.

- Talk about your commitment to him and the plans for seeing him.

- Take responsibility for the situation – it is usually a breakdown in feelings for both parties and an inability to resolve these.

- Do not confuse the child by continuing to occupy the same physical space; if you are separating then you must do so in order that he can begin to move on.

- The parent who has moved out should see the child in his new setting so that he can begin to formulate the meaning of the separation. Popping back to what was the family home will initially be very confusing for a child.

- Try to think about how hard it is for the adults to manage and then put yourself in the child's shoes. There is no point trying to pretend that this is not a temporarily destabilizing time. Admit to him that something very painful has happened, but also talk about how things will be under these new circumstances and stress any positives.

- Over time you and your ex-partner may be able to negotiate how you can come together to parent your child, but this resolution may be a long way down the line until you have both regained some stability in your lives.

Stepfamilies

Accommodating new members of the family is a delicate task. Often the adults will feel excited about a new partner and their children, but the children can have real concerns about the changes. In a society where stepfamilies are now more common, it may feel like a straightforward process, but a child won't have that overview at this point in her life.

A parent's happiness can come as quite a shock when it is in relation to a new partner. A new person, no matter how nice, can feel like an intruder to a child, or a threat to the comfortable situation she knows. So she may show a range of behaviours in order to communicate her feelings – such as being quite withdrawn, upset or, conversely, she might seem very pleased. This happiness might be genuine, but it could also be a way of masking her true feelings of hostility and resentment. I suppose what I am saying is, don't treat your child's initial response as the whole truth:

○ Start to talk to your child about any plans to change the make up of her family. Do this separately and then with your new partner to show that you are united.

○ Start slowly by introducing everyone and allowing space for each person to say how she finds these changes.

○ Don't condemn your child's worries – listen and think about what she is saying; often she will have a real fear that she will be forgotten.

○ Think carefully about what can be managed by both the adults and the child; it may be that you need to continue to live separately until everyone can cope with the change.

○ Talk to the other ex-partners about what is happening – especially if they are having contact with the child. No child should be put in the position of having to explain new arrangements to her parent.

○ Remember that most children will at some level find this very difficult and it will take time for them to adjust.

Dealing with the unexpected

Not everything can be predicted. There will be times when you will have to deal with issues as they arise and without being able to prepare for them, and in such situations you will need to help your child to do the same.

Instead of living in a constant state of panic and anxiety when something unforeseen occurs, help him to cope by being completely honest with him about what has happened and explain that it has come about unexpectedly. Be open about how you are feeling and give him space to share his feelings. Try not to give him the impression that things always happen in this way, but try to help him to understand that we cannot always know what is before us and that individuals are quite resilient and will get through these changes.

Bereavement

This issue falls into a very complex place. Adults themselves often find it extremely difficult to make sense of death, and so of course you can expect that children will also need help to deal with quite confused feelings about loss. They may not be able to understand what it means not to see someone again and thus they will be uncertain of what has happened.

Again, being honest about how you feel will allow your child to be more expressive about her feelings.

○ Talk about the person who has died and allow your child to reflect on things about him or her that hold meaning for her.

○ Do not make the mistake of trying to hide either pictures or memorable objects, as you risk creating a sense that death is associated with something very bad.

○ Use whatever spiritual explanation you believe in to help explain what has happened, but don't force this idea on your child. She will be really grappling with a concrete view that someone has disappeared and initially she doesn't truly understand what this means.

Family illness

Which family member it is who is ill will determine, in part, the impact on a child. If there is an ongoing illness then decisions need to be made about how he will visit, and continue to have a relationship with, that member of the family. Talk about

Be your child's rock

How a child responds to her parents very much depends on how safe she feels with them and how reliable she believes them to be. Make home life as consistent and stable as possible and you will provide opportunities for development and growth for all the family. As children grow up they rely on the situations around them to teach them how they should behave and they rely on our feedback to guide them.

the illness to children under ten years old in general terms; children a little older may be able to take in slightly more information. Use other adults to give you, as a parent, the support you need. Don't lean on your children, as this will put too much pressure on them and make them feel more burdened.

Tackling the issues

With all the parents I meet I try to establish a benchmark – something that we can all work towards together that seems reasonable and achievable. Being a 'good enough' parent is, for me, an important way of talking about parenting because I feel very strongly that wanting to be a super parent can often lead us to miss what is really required – which is to make sure that everyone in a family feels thought about and loved.

Parents can unwittingly become quite organized around visual trappings (for example, presents and 'things') rather than remembering that children want to feel that their parents love them, are proud of them and enjoy being with them. A hug, a positive comment, or both, are just what a child needs to feel that her parents care.

When you think about the issues you are having with your child, consider your own strengths and difficulties and the way you deal with her. (See pages 10–12 on the impact of your behaviour.) If you're not a morning person and you know you might be more crotchety at that time, be aware of the possible negative interactions that you may have with your child. Think about what really winds you up so you can be ready for these occasions and do not fly off into a rage when they happen.

Being prepared can pay real dividends and can head off all sorts of flashpoints where it feels like all your hard work has been undone. So if you are not a morning person, think about how you can avoid the things that press your buttons. Perhaps you could help your child to get her school/ nursery bag packed the night before and put her clothes out ready for her to put on? You could do the same for yourself, too. This preparation may make mornings far less stressful for everyone.

There will be other situations that can trigger potential difficulty that are personal to you; so think about what these flashpoints might be and then think about how you might anticipate them so that you can avoid any issues or confrontations. Then, whatever the situation, when you know that you are heading for a particular flashpoint, stop for a moment.

- Think: are you getting cross because of something that has happened to you which has put you in a bad mood, or because you are feeling under the weather?

- The more predictable you can be in your responses the easier it will be for your child, so make requests that she is used to and expect standards that have been agreed by both of you.

- If you change the rules without telling others be prepared for disappointment. Prepare your child and make sure she always knows what you expect from her.

- If you find that you are constantly complaining about your child or becoming enraged you are probably asking her to do something she is not capable of.

O Talk to your child about why you become cross to see if she understands your frustration.

O If you miss the signs of a flashpoint looming you will have to accept it – do not put this further frustration on to your child. Accept responsibility and move on.

Let's get down to the nitty gritty...

So now it's time to get back to basics and look at how you can begin to address your child's behaviour. We've taken into account some key life events and their impact on you and your child – now it's down to you.

Before we go on in this book and deal with specific behavioural problems and situations, read the following questions and use them to get an insight into you as a parent and the way that you behave in certain situations with your children:

What type of parent are you?

☐ Controlling.

☐ Fair.

☐ Firm.

☐ Warm.

☐ Easily irritated.

☐ Easy going.

Where are your strengths?

- ☐ Good listener.
- ☐ Fair but firm.
- ☐ Good at setting boundaries.
- ☐ Good at problem-solving.
- ☐ Good communicator.

In what areas do you feel that you need to develop?

- ☐ Your ability to stay calm.
- ☐ Listening and not taking sides.
- ☐ Putting yourself in your child's shoes.
- ☐ Admitting when you have got things wrong.
- ☐ Being clear about what you expect.
- ☐ Being consistent.

If you are a parent who can be overly controlling, how does this impact on your child?

Parents who are overly controlling leave very little to chance. They are often the parents who forget to listen to what their child wants – from which friend he has back for a play date, to whether or not he wants to go to a friend's party.

In my experience you can easily spot a child who is heavily controlled: he is the one who has little power over decisions in his life and who will be crying out for the opportunity to express himself through choices that he has made that are relevant to him and his interests.

So how do you know if you are too controlling?

Take the example of wanting your child to be popular and organizing play dates that they simply do not want. You will notice that a child often looks completely cut off at the thought of having another child over, when in actual fact all she wants is to come home and play and not feel that she has to accommodate someone else. Another similar situation might be that you are choosing activities that you want your child to do because you would have liked to have do them, even though week after week she objects to doing them.

Listen to your child – and if you did not get a request from her or a show of interest when you first suggested something the chances are that she does not want to be involved in it.

It can be incredibly difficult to allow things to just happen, and I completely understand why parents want to make sure that things are well planned and executed. However, the impact on a child of an existence that is so defined and controlled cannot be ignored. Think about how she would view the world if everything followed a regimented set pattern, where nothing was left to chance. How would she develop skills such as being flexible and adaptive?

I'm not saying that routines are not important, of course they are – they provide reliability and structure which can make a child feel very safe. Routines such as coming home from school, getting changed, having a snack, relaxing and completing homework before dinner are sensible. However, when other spontaneous activities cannot be entertained simply because children always have to have dinner at 5 p.m., then I would suggest that parents have slightly lost the plot.

Another example of the importance of being flexible is when your children go to their friends' houses. I can remember being told by one parent about a play date that she had set up where the other child's parent expected her son to eat at 5 p.m. and do his homework. Some play date – it sounded more like child-minding to me!

Don't forget, it can be such fun for a child to do something different and it is so important to teach children the need to be flexible.

So is there a problem?

As your child grows and matures you will see him exhibit a range of behaviours that you might not have seen before. Sometimes these are a natural part of growing up, exploring and experimenting, and they will vanish as suddenly as they appeared. But sometimes these behaviours are the result of other issues and changes going on in his life and might need more attention and investigation by the parent. In these situations it is up to the parent to decide whether the behaviour the child is displaying is acceptable to them and those around them, or whether it needs addressing before it escalates, or simply to help it stop.

The 'golden rule' with all of these questions is to be guided by your own instincts. Parents often know when something is wrong. However, if you are not comfortable with trusting your own instincts, speak to family or close friends to get a little more insight into the situation and to see if they also think there is an issue. Listen to them and other people around you if they are worried about the way in which your child is developing, and don't be defensive about their comments.

If you still aren't sure, talk to a health visitor or your GP, who should be able to give you a little more guidance. General issues to do with development can be reliably checked with them; these professionals can help put your mind at rest or indicate that a referral to further discuss the issues is needed.

The key factor in determining whether there is a behavioural problem is to know your own mind and to know your child. If you think there is a problem, but you can't think of any obvious event or change that might have triggered this new behaviour, ask yourself some of the following questions and see if the answers can help you get to the bottom of what's causing his unwanted behaviour:

- How much sleep is my child having?
- Should I cut down on naps in the day?
- Is my child eating enough?
- Is my child's speech developing at the correct rate?
- Which tantrums should I ignore and which ones should I respond to?
- Should I get worried when my children argue?

So let's deal with a few of these core issues.

Sleep

This is an area that always seems to tax parents. Typical sleep times for children should be:

Under 2 years	13 plus hours; this includes naps during the day.
2–3 years	12–13 hours; including naps of up to one and a half hours.
4–5 years	11–11½ hours; this is usually night-time sleep, as children are no longer napping.
6–9 years	10–10¾ hours.
10–12 years	9–9½ hours.

Of course these are just guidelines and some children will sleep a little less or a little more. If you feel that your child is not getting enough sleep and seems unsettled because of it, see your health visitor or GP for advice.

Eating

How much and how often a child should eat are really common questions. I have watched whole families agonize over a child who will not eat. I've seen them threaten and state very clearly that nothing else will be offered if she doesn't eat what's in front of her, only to hear or see the same child later sitting with some other food because the parents are so worried about her going hungry. I appreciate that, although it seems obvious this is not the right thing to be doing, sticking to your guns is really tricky because it is down to the parents to help their children develop healthy eating habits. This is an area that requires careful attention. So:

O Make sure that you are not giving your child portions that are too big.

O Allow your child enough time to eat – but anything more than an hour is too long.

O Offer help if it is needed.

O Praise any small developments, especially if your child tries something new.

O Don't allow a situation to happen where everyone in the family focuses on the child with difficulties.

O Be clear about the consequences of not eating in a straight-forward way, such as if she doesn't eat her dinner then she cannot have desert or treats later.

O Everyone should eat the same meal.

O Do not offer alternatives when the meal is finished. You want your child to understand that a consequence of not eating is that she may feel slightly hungry. (I can assure you that if you stick to this the problem will not go on for long.)

Development of speech

As children's speech and language skills develop, parents will often see quite wide variations in their children's ability, and it can be hard not to panic and compare your child with others of the same age. So to put your mind at rest, in general, this is what you should expect from him at various ages:

6–12 months

Children enjoy music, can understand far more than they can say and can respond to statements such as 'show me'.

12–24 months

Children begin to develop a small vocabulary and can use simple sentences such as 'there is a car'. Children also enjoy being read to at this age and can join in with nursery rhymes.

2–3 years

Children's sentence development is more apparent and they can repeat and make actions for nursery rhymes. They can also follow commands, for example, 'put the car on the box'.

4 years

Children's speech can be understood and they can form more elaborate sentences which describe activities or events they have been involved in. Children can also now refer to people that are not present.

5 years

Children will have a vocabulary of 1,500-plus words; they will know some colours, some facts about where they live and their parents' names.

6 years

Children love telling jokes at this age and will be able to have more adult-like conversations. They can also use language to express upset and can problem-solve, although their logic is not always clear to adults.

Trying to keep all of this information in your head and guide yourself and your child through the maze of child development is a full-time job. Remember that you are only human and you will get lots of things right and lots of things wrong as you guide your child towards adulthood.

Being a parent involves following a steep learning curve which often seems to keep on going up and up and up. This may sound ominous, but weigh it up against what your hard work will achieve: you will bring into society a balanced individual who will make a positive contribution. That has to make it all worthwhile.

Don't forget

○ Have high expectations of your child's behaviour – if you don't then he will not know what you expect of him.

○ You are the role model for your child. If you behave in a controlled and thoughtful way then the chances are that he will too.

○ Keep an eye on yourself. Imagine that you are being filmed and ask yourself what you would think about the way you are behaving.

○ Plan ahead. Try to predict some of the more tricky times when you know you won't be feeling your best and put on an act and be prepared. It is not acceptable to take your frustrations out on your child.

○ Your child is developing and, like a river, his development will move backwards and forwards. There are no hard and fast rules about each stage: they simply act as signposts for his development.

○ Think about how you respond to the things that life throws at you. Your child needs to learn how unpredictable life can be and how to deal with this unpredicatbility.

○ Be confident – know your own mind and trust your instincts. If you think your child is developing well, this is probably the case.

Don't let behaviour get you down

Stress has different guises: there's a healthy sort of stress we all need which drives us forward – increasing our performance and making us alert to our environment – but there is also a type of stress which gradually wears us down and makes us feel that we cannot perform even some of the most basic tasks. This is the stress that detrimentally affects our health and, inevitably, the way we relate to others.

Nowadays we all lead busy lives, and this contributes to a more compressed lifestyle for many families and myriad situations that can be deemed stressful. A typical day for lots of families will consist of the parent (or parents) going to work, children being taken to nursery, the child-minder or school until they are picked up and brought home. When they get home the children might eat with their parents and spend a little time as a family. In modern society our extended family often lives some distance away and grandparents are not around to help look after children, so parents increasingly have to do this job without the support our parents came to expect.

So with the pressures of modern living, how do we manage?

Think about the different situations you find yourself in every day; do you think you are coping with the stresses and strains of life as a parent? How can you avoid the reactive behaviour pattern that many of us fall into? By this I mean, have you developed a style of behaviour where you do not give yourself time to think about what you are doing? Do you instead just react in a rather robotic way to whatever is facing you? All parents should give themselves the time to think about their actions when in situations with their children and to reflect on them so that they can actively develop their parenting skills.

I regularly meet parents who have the best intentions. They have dreamt of having children and of being a parent; they have mulled over the positive and negative aspects of their own childhood experiences and from this they have made decisions about where and how they might do some things differently with their own family.

This kind of conclusion is an excellent starting point, but parents can come unstuck when reality strikes and they actually have a child and start to experience the different emotional pulls of being a parent, partner and an individual in their own right.

How many of us look forward to the end of the school day, the time when you are reunited with your child? The picture that parents conjure up in their heads is often not the picture that greets you. I have stood at many school gates, both as a parent and as a professional, and witnessed the very tricky interactions that are managed. So, with this in mind, how can parents find the tools to help them cope?

Make time work for you, not against you

Time is something that we all say that we do not have enough of, but if you maximize the little that you have then you can begin to ease the strain on yourself and your family.

Spend some time prioritizing what it is that you need to do and when. This will allow you to visualize your day and give you a framework within which to operate. This might sound like a tedious job, but a day can pass very quickly and you can keep stress levels down if you make the most of the time you have with the children and the time you have for yourself.

Each and every one of us wants to be the best parent we can be. Realistically, though, there are only going to be a few times when, at the end of the day, you can give yourself a pat on the back and say you had the day that you wanted to have. There are probably going to be more times when you definitely will not feel this way, so what I am trying to stress here is that once you recognize that parenting has good bits and bad bits, the job becomes easier.

Pace yourself

The key to making time work for you rather than against you is about prioritizing the things you need to get done, and perhaps even not doing some things that really aren't necessary.

The big question you need to ask yourself is: what are you trying to achieve? Sit down at the beginning of the week and consider what you want to get done in the week ahead. While you are doing this, think about which of these things can wait and which really do not need to be attended to immediately. The list might include: picking the children up from school, having school friends back, after-school activities, doing the shopping, cleaning, etc. Then at the end of the week, review how everything went; make a note of any activities that didn't happen and see if you can include them in the plan for the following week.

Keep doing this, week by week, and soon you should start to discover a healthy balance and response to what is happening and what needs to happen. Be realistic with your expectations: if you continue to set yourself unmanageable targets then you are leaving yourself open to feeling a failure.

So take a look at which jobs are actually getting done and which need to be done every day. Ask yourself whether any of the things that are consistently being forgotten do in fact need to be done, or if you can delegate them to someone else or get some help with them. Perhaps your partner or older children can do their bit with domestic chores, or perhaps the finances might stretch to pay for a cleaner, or perhaps you could have the weekly shopping delivered to save you the job.

Take a look at what your children are doing, too, and see if there is scope to scale down their after-school activities. You might be surprised to discover that they are often just as happy to go home when the school day ends and spend some time chatting to you, watching a television programme as a family, or even just having some free time to themselves at home to play with their toys or be in their own space.

Reducing the demands on everyone at the end of a long day can be a very rewarding way for you to give yourselves time to spend together, and this will undoubtedly help reduce your levels of unhealthy stress.

Share your concerns

Talking about how you are coping is really important. Many of us chat to family and friends when challenging situations emerge at work, so it always surprises me that parents worry about taking time to talk about issues they are facing at home. It is almost as if it is a deadly sin to be struggling with family life. Parents often feel judged by other parents and thus they start to feel that they have to keep quiet about the issues they are facing.

Remember, no-one is perfect; we could all do with a little help to check out how we are doing. Some people find it helpful to talk to someone one-on-one, while others prefer to discuss things as part of a group.

In essence, the job of parenting is a delicate balancing act, so give yourself the opportunity to talk about what is on your mind and then, as the saying goes, a problem shared is a problem halved.

Make sure the children don't lose out

How would you react if someone at work was trying to do loads of tasks at the same time as explaining to you how to do something that is central to your job? You probably wouldn't put up with this and you would expect to be given a little more attention; I believe that our children also send us very clear messages when they think they are being short-changed.

Some of our problems arise from the minimal amount of time that we give ourselves to get everything done at work and at home whilst also looking after our children. Multi-tasking is something that becomes second nature to busy parents; how often do you find you're cooking the dinner, arranging after-school activities on the telephone, unpacking a school bag and completing the dreaded homework – all at the same time? An achievement, yes, but what makes parents feel that this whirl of activity is acceptable to, or appreciated by, their children? Alongside this scenario you will often find a disgruntled child who feels that there is no space to express himself, and so whatever he says or does to get his parents' attention is responded to angrily or in an offhand way.

In order to achieve a harmonious home and a happy family you need to make time for your children – no matter how busy you are. If you work, or if your children are at school, or you find it hard to give them time during the day, then decide on and set aside some special time at the beginning or end of every day – whatever fits best with your routine. In that time – half an hour, an hour, whatever you can spare – try to focus completely on your child and give him your undivided attention. Perhaps you could eat breakfast with him, or dinner, help him with his homework or read him a bedtime story.

If you have more than one child, try to spend special time with each one separately – be it doing homework, taking him out or sitting on the sofa with him and chatting. Make it a regular thing so he knows he will get this time to be with you and he will be able to communicate his concerns or problems without any interruptions from the phone or other members of the family. (See Chapter 4 for more advice on this.)

Feeling in control

When you have children it can take some time until you feel that you have regained your adult self. Being a parent can make you feel as if you have lost a lot of skills, and the stability and predictability that you felt before you were responsible for someone else's every need can very quickly seem to be being eroded.

Each stage of development that a child goes through brings with it another huge learning curve for her parents. Just as we begin to get through the sleepless nights, so comes your child's fight for independence, followed by her wish to be given the freedom that a teenager dreams of.

So how can you maintain a feeling of being in control and having a reasonable grip on being a parent? In order to have a sense of control you need to be able to feel that you can think clearly and that other people will respond to and respect your decisions. When you've had a baby it is these feelings that often no longer seem to be areas of certainty.

Start as you mean to go on; take control and make key decisions when you feel yourself getting stronger:

O Initially, have a loose plan for the day. If you still have a young baby you will need to plan trips or visitors around her sleep times – don't be forced into working around other people's timescales.

O Gradually try to build up a routine of getting up in the morning and getting yourself ready. You will find that the more ordinary routines you establish at this stage, the more confident you will feel.

O When you feel ready to have some time for yourself, begin to have short breaks away from your baby. This will act as a test for both of you to see how you manage.

O As time moves on and your baby's behaviour becomes a bit more predictable, try to rekindle interests that you had before you became a parent so that you feel like a person in your own right once more.

When your life and events around you feel unpredictable it is a real help to have some structures in place which make parts of your life feel more stable. Creating a rhythm and a routine to your life, particularly when you have a new baby, is a really good way of giving yourself a sense of being in control and should make you feel less stressed.

Get off the merry-go-round...

One of my patients once said to me, 'Functioning as an adult seemed so straightforward before children.' I completely agree. Children suddenly turn an often predictable world into a whirling merry-go-round – at least until you manage to get off and begin to take control again.

Being an adult in the workplace, and away from home and your children, can afford you a little thinking time and space to solve problems and make plans. This breathing space is precious to a parent who has no time to think about, and so only space to react to, issues at home.

So in order to regain control of your home life, you need to use some of the same approaches to parenting that you use in your working life. Prioritize what you need to get done (see pages 48–9); give yourself the time that you would demand at work; and don't be forced into making instant decisions about how to handle something. There is nothing wrong with juggling a handful of balls – it's just that every so often one should be allowed to fall so you can give it the attention it needs. Remember, letting something go – even temporarily – isn't failing, it's giving yourself time to do it properly.

Inevitably there are different approaches to parenting. Some parents like to have a really hands-on style, where they manage the children between themselves; some have help and support to fill the gaps; and others believe that, after a certain stage, their children should, and are able to, function fairly independently without too much input from them.

For working parents, or those with other commitments of caring for sick relatives or other children, balancing these responsibilities with their home life can prove an almighty headache – particularly when you stop and look at friends and family around you and begin to compare and contrast what they are doing with what you have to manage.

No one of these parenting styles is the only answer. How you approach your role as a parent should depend on your personal situation. Do you share childcare with a partner? Do you work part-time or full-time? Do you have willing family members who happily help with the children?

You need to think about your own situation and remember that everyone's situation is unique. In reality, there's no point comparing yourself with others because individual values and thoughts are often very different. Don't let other people make you feel guilty for the decisions and arrangements that you

Work day? Or play day?

If you are a working parent, help your child understand how the week is structured by making timetables that show where everybody will be. Use language like 'mummy not at work' and 'mummy's work day' to highlight where the changes are. Include both parents in this. If the father is out at work for longer hours, writing 'reading with daddy' on the timetable will create an idea in your child's mind of how her parents work together to look after her. You'll be amazed at how quickly children start to remind you which day is which, and it should act as a good reminder, and hopefully a spur, for parents to prioritize their children's needs over work.

Children grow up very quickly, and they will remember these moments together forever.

make to look after your children; the most important factor in these choices is that your child is happy.

Remember too that children will adapt to whatever situation they find themselves in. If parents are comfortable with the childcare provisions they have made then it is highly likely that the child will also be happy with, and will cope with, these arrangements.

There are some fundamental principles that can be followed by everyone (regardless of your home or work situation) that will help restore the balance between family and other responsibilities:

- Make the most of the time that you do have.

- Arrange a time when you expect everyone to be at home and spend it doing something together. You may play a game together, or just relax watching a film with some snacks; the key is not to turn this into another time-pressured space, but to enjoy each other's company.

- Monitor how much time you are spending at home finishing things off for work and decide whether you think this is acceptable or whether it could be reduced.

- Eat meals together whenever possible.

- Give yourselves relaxation times together – just sitting on the sofa gives everyone time to recharge their batteries.

- Ask your children what they like doing and observe them; e.g. if PlayStation is the latest craze watch them play a game and comment on how skilful they are. All too often praise for our children's talents or skills are discussed amongst adults when really it is our children who need to hear how proud we are of them.

○ Make bedtimes a sacred time when you are available exclusively to your children for at least 45 minutes.

○ Limit telephone calls to when the children are in bed.

Remember, don't spoil or indulge your child out of guilt. Children are astute enough to realize the difference between a genuine gesture and something that is manufactured. Any indulgence you choose to give them should include more elements from the ordinary fabric of family life, which includes lots of physical affection and love shown through spending time together.

However, in this family time together don't be lulled into relaxing the structures you have put in place to help your family to function – rules and boundaries still apply. For example, keep to your agreed bedtimes and do not accept behaviour from your children that you would not usually tolerate just because it is 'special time'.

I believe that all these things are fundamental building blocks in showing your child your appreciation and love for him. In this way, as he gets older and he naturally wants to assert his independence, he will know that he is part of a family which is willing to make time for him and will always look after him.

If you let your child know that he can opt in and out of the family (within agreed limits!), this flexibility will ultimately give him the tools that he needs to deal with a variety of complex situations. And, equally importantly, learning to manage your time and your priorities will give you space to breathe, relax and enjoy your children, which in turn will make parenting a less stressful and more fulfilling, happy experience!

Don't forget

O Monitor your stress levels, take action and use the time available to you to plan ahead.

O Organization is key. Question what is a priority and make lists of what really needs doing, then decide to delay or give up any unnecessary activities/chores.

O Get help if/where you can.

O Make time to relax with your family; replace hectic schedules with an evening in.

O Find people to talk to with whom you can share what is on your mind.

Taming tantrums

For me, tantrums are one of the most arresting of all the behaviours that children throw at us. Imagine the scene: a family are out shopping; everyone seems fine and happy until you tell your toddler that it's time to leave and, without any warning, a noise emerges from her like you have never heard before or thought possible. 'What happened? Where did it all go wrong?' I hear you cry. This is a scene that is witnessed time and time again, and whenever I see it my heart goes out to the parent who is standing there, completely flabbergasted.

When children let rip

Tantrums are a child's way of expressing his most intense feelings when he is unable to verbalize them. Children have different ways of showing their frustration: some shout and scream; others bite, scratch and hit out; and others may throw objects, such as toys – or, in fact, anything they can get their hands on could be hurled through the air.

Interestingly, parents seem to have different 'comfort zones' when it comes to reacting to tantrums. They might find that there are certain behaviours they can ignore, while others really push their buttons and send them into an internal frenzy. Remember the Incredible Hulk, when all the fluids in his body start to react and he turns green with rage? I have had parents relive with me how angry they become when their child explodes into a tantrum and reveal that they feel their children have the ability to turn them into such monsters too!

Indeed, there are certainly some behaviours that many parents feel more comfortable with than others, and they will all touch us differently. Usually parents are more worried when their children hurt themselves, other children or them. This kind of behaviour can bring a different level of anxiety to parents because they will be concerned about why their child is behaving in this way and what he is trying to communicate through these actions.

So what's it all about?

A child uses a tantrum to let us know that something is wrong and that she needs help to resolve the way she is feeling or thinking: for example, how upset, frustrated, angry, jealous, scared, ill, tired or hungry she is.

It is quite normal for toddlers between the ages of one and three to have tantrums because, with their limited verbal communication skills, this is one way they are able to express strong emotions (see Chapter 1). Although tantrums are common behaviour amongst toddlers, there is a lot of variation – some children have a lot of tantrums, others have very few.

Children use tantrums to demonstrate their frustration – most often it will be down to wanting something that they cannot have. It's almost as if children have a special button that says, 'If I cannot get what I want I will find another way.' Of course, this behaviour is not just confined to toddlers; children of all ages will use this tactic to see if it gets results.

Mirroring behaviour

Tantrums bring a range of responses from parents. However, when you are stuck in the moment with your child all the rules about how to react go out of the window. I've often thought how strange it must look to a child when he is in the throes of a tantrum to look up and to see his parent screaming back at him. If someone filmed that situation, how would it look to you? I'm guessing it wouldn't look great and you might wonder who was behaving badly – the adult or the child?

Mirroring your child's behaviour doesn't only happen when you are reacting to his tantrum: how many of us can put up our hands and say that we haven't momentarily (or longer) had a paddy and really behaved in an unacceptable manner? How we behave does have a direct influence on our children, and they will use this as an example of how to behave.

A colleague of mine once went to observe a child in a nursery because the staff there were concerned about her speech development and explosive behaviour. The little girl was trying to unscrew a bottle top and as she struggled she turned around and said, 'I can't get the bloody thing off!' She then threw it down and went off to start another activity. Whenever she became frustrated her behaviour became more unmanageable until eventually she had a tantrum and pushed another child over. It's not rocket science to imagine how some of the adults in her world dealt with frustration. They certainly had not presented her with a helpful template for her own behaviour.

As children grow and face new situations, they need to find out how to get what they want in order to gain some control over their environment. When this is not possible they have to find a way to release the tension that they are feeling, and this happens through the only means they know – a tantrum.

It might not seem possible, but tantrums provide parents with an opportunity to teach their child about her responses. Just as adults have to manage themselves in testing times, so children need to learn to do this too. So instead of thinking about this as a completely awful time, think of it as a chance to help your child to develop her resilience and her ability to cope with upset.

Watch and learn

When you see your child having a tantrum, what do you think? It is important to have some questions about what is happening, as finding answers to these will help you to slow the situation down, give yourself some thinking time and plan your response. Remember, behaviour is a powerful communication: everything we do is for a reason. So think carefully, what is your child trying to tell you?

At its most basic level a tantrum is designed to have maximum impact and to get your attention. Perhaps your child is demanding this attention because he feels tired, hungry or unwell? If this is the case we would all want to make ourselves available to our child in order to show him that we are there to care for him.

But, here are a few 'golden rules' when it comes to dealing with tantrums:

● Don't react to tantrums without thinking about the message you are sending; are you rewarding his bad behaviour by giving him attention? If you do respond to his tantrum, rather than ignore it, tell him clearly that you are doing so because you can see that he is upset and you want to help.

● Tell your child that you want him to show some control before you will respond to his request.

● Remind him that there are other ways to communicate his feelings. It is better for everyone if he just comes to you to tell you what the matter is.

● Try to notice what triggers your child's tantrum, where it happens and whether there is a regular pattern.

● Look out for subtle changes in his mood. Does he seem more irritable than usual? Do the tantrums happen when he is hungry, exhausted or overexcited?

● Who is most often around when these tantrums happen?

● Think about whether or not you are behaving differently when the tantrums occur. Are you particularly stressed or tired at the moment? Or are you perhaps more short tempered than usual?

● When you have managed to calm or stop a tantrum, what did you do? If a particular strategy has worked, perhaps you could try this again another time.

● Whatever you do, remember that no parent can prevent tantrums happening every time.

Typical reasons for tantrums

Tantrums often rear their ugly heads when a child has few problem-solving skills. Most toddlers do not talk very much; they have trouble asking for things in a straightforward way and have difficulty expressing themselves verbally. Parents need to be conscious of this and know that their child is not behaving in this way on purpose – she simply has no other way of getting her feelings across.

As children get older and start to attend school, they have better communication skills and better coping strategies to manage frustrating situations. Tantrums will still occur as a way of expressing upset or disappointment, but much less frequently. In fact, depending on how parents have managed the tantrum phase, at this age a child should be developing more sophisticated ways of self-expression.

If a child has learnt that having a tantrum is a quick way of getting something that she wants, she now has the ability to be conscious of her actions. The average four-year-old will think about how much fuss she needs to create in order to get what she wants. However, often a quick reminder from a parent, for example, 'I'm not going to speak to you until you stop behaving like that,' has the desired effect, as she will have learnt that you really will not give in. Be consistent in your response and, when she is around four years old and above, you will see that this helps to stop a large number of tantrums.

Still unsure about why your child is behaving this way? Here are some other common reasons for tantrums:

Not getting their own way

This is a tricky problem; I have met adults who struggle when they don't get their own way and who are an absolute nightmare to be around. Thankfully, most adults have moved on from throwing themselves around the room and stamping their feet!

Young children find not getting their own way a real shock; especially if they are only children or have siblings who are easy going. Similarly, if you as a parent have worked hard to smooth over potential conflicts, suddenly finding you cannot have your own way is a very big surprise. There are some things you must expect from your children: they will have battles over possessions or wanting something done their way. Children have to learn to share and at first they will find the feelings that go with sharing difficult, but the more they practise, the better it gets (see Chapter 4).

As a parent what you say and do in response to this behaviour is instrumental in helping your child to find alternative ways to react. If you acknowledge how difficult it is for him to share and praise him whenever he does, your child can and will learn that the world will not collapse if he doesn't get his own way.

Set up situations where your child has to share his toys, your attention or treats. If your child objects to sharing, say that you know it is hard but encourage him to give the toy to the other person for a short time; this way he will begin to see that he can get things back. Invite some of his friends round;

then stay with the children whilst they are playing and keep encouraging them to work together to solve any problems that arise from one person wanting to have his own way.

Upset over a new sibling

This can be a very upsetting situation. The extent to which it develops into a problem is dependent on a number of factors: your responses, your child's position in the family, the age gap between the children and also their gender.

If you put in the work at the beginning I believe that a lot of the problems can be headed off before they start (see Chapter 2). For example, if you have a son who is planning for a baby brother before the baby is born, this is the time to create an alternative picture so that he begins to see that the sex of his new sibling is not something you can fix. Be aware of your own conversations about the new baby (which can often be over-heard by your other children). If you are hoping the baby will be a certain sex you can hardly blame your child for wishing the same. Statements made even in passing can lead children to believe this is what you want and thus it will happen.

Prepare your child for a new sibling by talking openly about what it will be like at first, i.e. that the baby will need lots of your attention. You could get your child to think about how she can help. Explain that you will have to find some special times together and make a list of what you will do together. Take seriously your child's concerns about how the time you have for her will be different and her worries about having to share

your attention. These are all realities, so don't sweep them under the carpet. Gently acknowledge to your child that things will be different for a while, but that very soon she will have more of your time and a brother or sister to play with too.

Change

Everyone struggles with change, be it planned or unplanned, and in many ways this is natural. However, when change produces a prolonged, extreme emotional reaction, such as 'I'm not budging', this should be challenged.

Talk to your child as soon as you know about a change, and if something happens that was unplanned let him know this was the case. Tell your child that you understand that he is upset but that this change will happen and you need his help to get through it. Perhaps talk to him about what he can do to help. For example, if he is moving into a new room he could think about what he would like to take with him, how he would like to change the room, decorate it, and so on.

Always pick up on the positive aspects of the change to help your child see what is ahead in a different light.

General frustration

How often do you see children fall into a tantrum when really they are just frustrated? Teaching children different ways to manage their frustration is hard, so until they can do so, try to anticipate these feelings. There will be times when you are near to your child and you will hear her begin to struggle with something, so let her know you have noticed her frustration. A reassuring comment shows that you have noticed how hard she is trying or how hard something is. This can be really helpful, because by acknowledging her effort you are signalling to your child that some things are more difficult than others, but that it is worth persevering.

You might want to offer your child a helping hand if she is struggling, which will show her that you are always available to help. Letting children know that you are there if they need you will help them hold on to the idea that sometimes when things feel a little bit tricky they can ask for help. This is an invaluable lesson for life.

Know when to offer help

Pick your moment as to when to step in and offer help to your struggling child, but you can usually tell by his response whether your help is appreciated. Don't just wade in, as this will make him feel you're highlighting his difficulties, and don't take over. Instead, show him how to solve the problem; for example, if he is trying to cut paper, demonstrate by using another bit of paper and encourage your child to copy you.

A quick statement such as 'I'm here if you want me to help' can also give your child the space to make a decision about when and how he asks for help, and this in turn will make him feel more in control of the situation.

Extreme tantrums

There are times when a child gets himself into such a state while having a tantrum that he canake himself physically sick. This is a terribly distressing situation and one in which parents have to be on hand with a sympathetic response in case he is worried by what has happened.

Concentrate on calming him down: hold your child close to your chest and wait for his breathing to become more regular. Once he is calm, talk about what led to the tantrum and try to find a way to explain that you understand that he got very angry. Try to make your child see that he always has you to help him and that next time he should come and find you before he feels the need to have such a tantrum.

Just because the tantrum has been extreme, do not fall into the trap of feeling that you need to treat him or give in to his tantrum. If you do this he will realize that he is rewarded for this behaviour and he may be tempted to try it again.

What to do

When responding to a tantrum you are providing your child with a response that shows her how she can and cannot behave.

Respond to her screaming, kicking or hitting in a calm and consistent way – this approach is crucial even if you are seething inside and want to explode yourself! Keep angry thoughts in your head but present an external picture to your child of complete calm. This will provide her with some security whilst she is feeling so out of control.

I think that it is important for you to acknowledge what happens to you when your child is having a tantrum. Depending on where you are when the tantrum occurs, it can be very upsetting, embarrassing, disappointing, infuriating or irritating. You have to manage these feelings, otherwise there is a risk of communicating them to your child, which can lead to an acceleration in her tantrum, leaving her feeling that the situation is unsafe and that you cannot cope. Hold onto your feelings until you are able to find an opportunity to talk to someone else.

If tantrums occur on a relatively frequent basis, think about how to deal with them and formulate a plan with your partner, family or friends. Decide on a strategy that moves from the least intervention through to a more robust intervention on your part, and make sure that anyone who looks after the child knows your strategy and is willing to follow through on it if need be.

Below are the steps that will guide you through a series of interventions which graduate from the least intrusive to more intrusive.

Let's consider each one in turn:

Ignoring

Many tantrums can be ignored. Often a child's tantrum is simply designed to get your attention and when it receives no acknowledgement the tantrum will begin to die down as if extinguished by a bucket of water! So, as you become more familiar with your child's tantrums and you recognize that he is behaving in this way purely for attention, try to switch off and see what happens when you do not get involved. I always keep half an eye on my own children's behaviour and have a little smile to myself as they look at me as if to say, 'Well, do something then!' or, 'This doesn't seem to be working.'

Remind yourself that tantrums are designed to get your attention, and that ignoring them might make them stop. Don't be fooled into ignoring and then, when they start up again, getting involved. It is vital that you are consistent in ignoring them – unless the situation escalates and you think someone is about to get hurt.

Distraction

This is one of the most fantastic tools available to a parent; as a child begins to work herself into a tantrum, think of something to distract her. I have found that introducing an alternative game, book, or even suggesting that she follows you into a different room can often do the trick.

This technique is particularly effective with toddlers, so offer your child an alternative if she objects to having some-thing take away from her. Say clearly that she cannot have that thing but that she can have something else. Say why this is the case so she realizes that there is a reason for your actions. Congratulate your child if she accepts the alternative item that is on offer and demonstrate your pleasure with a hug and a kiss. This will help your child to feel that all is not lost and that you appreciate her flexibility.

Verbal comment

I would suggest that you use this approach when you feel that your child's behaviour is escalating and he needs to know that you are aware of this. Perhaps say something like, 'Is there something that I can help you with?' or, 'You need to stop making that noise now before I can talk to you.'

Alternatively, you might want to say something to him that acknowledges that the situation is starting to get out of hand such as, 'I can see you are getting angry. Now remember what we said, come and see me and let's think about how I might be able to help you.'

Remember, the more you verbalize what is happening, the easier it becomes for a child to notice what happens to him when he gets angry, and he may be able to stop himself by coming to you before things go too far.

Verbal comment that includes a prompt about a consequence

In many ways this is a comment that reminds your child what might happen if she continues. It might include a countdown, such as that by the time you have counted down from five you want her to stop or she will be given a time out (see page 77).

By alerting your child to a consequence you are helping her learn to take responsibility for her actions and basically letting her know that she has a choice about what happens next. You must always follow through if your child does continue to tantrum, but if she settles down you need to tell her that you know that she was angry and praise her for making the right choice.

If you are using a consequence, make sure you pick something that makes sense for your child, depending on her age:

○ Time out works well for children aged two upwards.

○ All children can be scared by a tantrum, so holding them

Keep tabs on tantrums

It can be very difficult to know from one day to the next whether what you are doing in response to tantrums is working, so keep a notepad where you record what seems to trigger a tantrum, who is around at the time and what happens. Note what you do in response so that you can get an idea as to whether ignoring your child works or whether this adds fire to the flames!

Having this sort of checklist will also help you notice whether or not you are consistent and will prevent you slipping into bad habits. Remember, a time out is only to be used when your child hits another child or throws things to hurt – you don't want to find yourself using this for every issue or it will lose its power.

Use the notes to check how providing reassurance and talking things through with your child helps her to calm down. You may find you are not doing enough of this and you need to balance out the range of responses that you are using.

on your lap until they calm down can be very reassuring; this can work with children up to five years old, too. (The holding I am talking about is not pinning your child to your lap but a firm cuddle that quickly moves into something more reassuring once she begins to calm down.)

Physical intervention

By physical intervention I do not mean physical punishment, such as smacking; this approach is merely about getting physically involved in a situation. This response should be a fairly well-rehearsed one for any behaviour that could lead to someone being hurt. I have always been very clear with all of my children that hitting will result in a consequence, such as a time out or time away from the rest of us. Many of you reading will know the general principle for time out. For those of you less familiar with this approach, it is as follows:

● Put your child in a safe and unstimulating setting for a short time. This can be a room or you can just use a chair.

● The length of time he should sit there should be calculated according to his age – using one minute for every year of his age. So, for example, a child of three should sit for three minutes, a four-year-old for four minutes, and so on.

● This can be a little messy at first, as your child will probably protest at being placed away from everybody, but persevere and soon you will find that this can be an incredibly helpful intervention that allows you to stay calm and away from further confrontation.

Time's up for time out

Once your child is five years old, the maximum amount of time you should apply to any timed out intervention is five minutes; anything more just does not work. So children aged five and over should all receive a just five-minute time out consequence – no more.

Stop it before it starts

Sometimes it is possible to head off a tantrum before it takes hold. In order to do this you need to look out for the signs that a tantrum is brewing:

- Listen: can you hear her beginning to get frustrated?
- Can you hear toys being banged about or an exchange of words indicating there will be an argument?
- Has it gone very quiet? This may be a sign that there is a struggle of some kind going on.

If you spot any of the signs above:

- Interrupt or intercept before a tantrum can take hold by causing a distraction.
- Remind your child that you are available to help resolve any issues.
- Be more present and help children to work together and to share, if that is the cause of a tantrum.
- Remove your child if the situation is becoming dangerous

(for example if toys are thrown or if she starts hitting others) and make sure there is a consequence for her behaviour.

What not to do

You need to keep a clear head to stop children from having tantrums. I have heard people say that children grow out of tantrums; parents play a huge role to help make this possible.

Negotiating with your child during a tantrum is not helpful. Some of the best interventions that I have observed (and I have seen a lot in my local shopping centre!) have been where parents have acted swiftly and without hesitation. Tell your child how you expect him to behave, and if this doesn't work, tell him what the consequence will be if he does not calm down. Children will either calm down in response or challenge their parents to follow through and so up the anti and begin to behave even more appallingly. Anyone who looks carefully at a parent's face whilst they are in the middle of such a scenario can see how painful it is to be dealing with this behaviour.

If your child is in the throes of a tantrum, there are two effective responses. First, if he calms down when asked to, it is vital that this is acknowledged and that you comment positively on it. You need to say how pleased you are with the way in which he stopped.

If, on the other hand, he won't stop and ups his tantrum then you have to stand firm. If you are out of your home, you can still give him a time out by getting him to stand for the allotted time (you may need to hold his hand to help him, but make sure you do not speak to him and that you withdraw all other attention). You may need to leave the shopping centre, or wherever else you are, to do this (carrying your screaming child) or return to the car if that is possible. It may feel humiliating, but you have to do it in the knowledge that this will help your child. Ignore all those judging faces and concentrate.

Getting involved in a conversation with him which will allow him to bargain with you while you try to persuade him out of his tantrum is a no-no: striking a bargain equals backing down.

Can you remember being in such a situation? On reflection, why do you think you responded in the way you did? The answer often centres around one of the following:

- You felt embarrassed.
- You don't like to see your child upset.
- You want a quiet life and a speedy end to the noise.

None of the above are good enough reasons for letting your child behave in an appalling way. Giving in is a short-term solution and it is really like putting a small plaster over a rather large cut – the problem won't go away unless it has the proper treatment.

There is a flip side to the reactions set out above, though. Keeping your head and not overreacting is essential. As with all interventions there are going to be times when you get it right and times when there is definitely room for improvement! It can take a massive effort to stay on track with your own

Let the show go on...

For some reason a tantrum usually seems to gain support for the child; well-meaning people often become involved in an attempt to look after the 'poor child'. When your child is acting up the added embarrassment of other people looking on can be excruciating. I have to confess that I've been guilty of watching children writhing around on the floor and have found myself wondering who has made this happen, only to gaze in the direction of the parent and to realize that this is the child's latest Oscar-winning performance! It seems to be a natural human response that when we hear a child crying we assume she has been wronged in some way.

I had a well-planned response to what was becoming an all-too frequent occurrence with one of my children when out shopping. We would be happily 'window shopping' only to be confronted with our child indulging herself with a screaming fit once we made it clear it was time to move on, followed by her lying on the floor. We had agreed to deal with this performance by ignoring it and moving away a few steps. One day we did this and all was going well until I heard a lady say, 'Ah, what's the matter, what do you want? Where are your mummy and daddy?' Well, that was the moment of triumph for my child, as I then had to walk back to the woman and explain that everything was OK and she need not worry.

In such a situation let those around you know that you have a plan that they need to let you carry out, and that you know this is the best response to your child's behaviour.

behaviour, but try to imagine how you must look to your child when you respond to his tantrum with one of your own. You are twice or three times your child's height and are probably making more noise than him while telling him that he should know better and that he needs to calm down. A sobering picture, I think you'll agree.

When will this stop?

As with other developmental stages, working through the tantrum stage seems endless and will take children different amounts of time. You might feel as if you have passed through this phase only to find your child having a series of mega tantrums at the slightest thing. If this is the case, review why you think she is behaving in this way. Remind yourself that this is a stage your child needs to go through and that the learning she takes on here will be invaluable in helping her to tolerate and manage frustration throughout her life.

Don't forget

O Tantrums are to be expected of very young children, so accept them as an important part of your child's development – but remember that you have the ability to anticipate them before they take hold and to take control.

O Remember your reflective stance. Assess the situation and consider the following, then you may be able to deal with tantrums almost instantly and have fewer of them:

⊙ Where and when do they happen?

⊙ What triggers them? Are there patterns that you haven't noticed?

⊙ Keep a careful watch and note what you observe.

O As tantrums are often about gaining control, try to make your child's day as predictable as possible. Think about how important it is to you to have routines; it is equally important for him to know what happens and when.

O Everyone wants to stay sane, so consider which battles are worth fighting over. If you have a child who frequently has tantrums then ignore the ones that don't involve someone else being hit or hurt in some way. Stop yourself from getting involved every time he has a tantrum, as this can be particularly rewarding for some children.

O Be there to support your child if he becomes frustrated; offer reassurance and support and try to divert the tantrum before it begins.

Getting along with others

So what are social skills?

A person's social skills centre on how they relate and interact with each other and how comfortable they feel in the company of one other person and/or a group. The development of this skill is a complex task for children.

As an adult you probably have a way of behaving that you know is acceptable in different situations. As I have mentioned in earlier chapters, I often think about what it would be like to watch myself on camera and how I would judge my own behaviour. I know that I act differently according to who I'm with or what I'm doing. For instance, my manner is much more relaxed when I am with my family, purely because of the amount of time that we spend together and the fact that we share a more intimate and informal relationship at home. Of course, in more formal, work-based settings our behaviour tends to be more reserved, socially acceptable and less 'risky', due to the different expectations that are placed upon us.

So we know that, as adults, we adapt our behaviour to make it appropriate to any given situation. This is something we have learned, and as we mature it becomes quite natural to many of us. Young children have all of this to learn – and it is quite a minefield. Just as they begin to understand how to operate and behave within their immediate family environment, they move outside of the home and into different settings; and this is when the rules change. They soon discover, for example, that what is OK at home is not OK at Grandma's, and what is fine at Grandma's is definitely not OK at nursery.

Preparing children for this subtle change is a difficult task, but one that is vitally important if they are to feel confident and happy in society.

What are we aiming for?

As parents we all want to know that our children are happy and comfortable amongst their friends and peers. Over the course of their lives they will experience a wide variety of relationships: from very close, intimate family relationships to more formal relationships with those people they meet at school, at work and in day-to-day life, and we want them to be successful in making and maintaining these relationships.

The key features we all hope that we and our children will possess are to be likeable, to be someone whose company others enjoy and to be a person who, on the whole, has the skills to get along well with others.

Right from the very beginning, as our children develop and grow, we parents watch to see how they relate to our family and friends in a variety of situations. As you read this you can probably remember the times that you or someone else has commented on how well your child was playing and interacting with other children. Comments like this will be heard with much pride (and relief!), as we all seem to think that how our child behaves socially forms one of the benchmarks for how successfully we have parented her, and how others perceive that we are parenting her.

So what can we realistically hope to achieve?

Encouraging good behaviour in a social setting is another key area in parenting where you are pivotal in helping your child to develop the 'right' code of conduct.

How many times have you found yourself in a situation where family or friends have asked you about your children and how they get along with each other? Whenever I am asked this I always feel that how I answer is somehow crucial to how I will be viewed as a parent. In fact, I often think this is a rather loaded question. So on the one hand I want to reply truthfully and say that my children get along fairly well but they have their moments, but on the other hand, in order to preserve my

Honesty is the best policy

One of my parents was told by her health visitor that she should always remember that our children make liars of us. By this she meant that parents should always tell the truth, otherwise our children will behave in a way that reflects the true situation, or they will blurt something out.

This is so true, and I have learnt that a truthful, balanced response as to how things genuinely are for you and your child is very important if you want to encourage good behaviour and open and honest communication with your child.

position as a 'good' parent, it is tempting to say that they get on perfectly well with no problems at all.

Sometimes an honest response will result in you being judged fairly harshly by others who might set their standards at a height that no-one can really meet.

It can be agonizing when you are out in public with your children and they behave in a way that you do not expect or do not want them to. Many of us try to pay particular attention to how our children behave and conduct themselves and so it can be incredibly upsetting when they behave in a way that you really are not happpy with, and it can even make you feel really 'let down'.

Children will generally pick up on their parents' disappointment, so it is important to make it clear to them why you are upset. Not talking about your feelings can leave a child unsure of what he has actually done wrong. So:

- Restate clearly what behaviour you expect from him.
- Single out the behaviour that you didn't like, making it clear that it is this that you are upset about. (It is important to name the behaviour so that your child is clear that you still love/like him; it's just the behaviour you're unhappy with.)
- Try to think about how he might behave differently next time, discuss it with him and let him know that this is what you will be expecting instead.
- If your child behaves differently next time, make sure you acknowledge and praise his improved behaviour as a way of reinforcing it.

What part can we play in this?

Clearly, we all behave in a variety of different ways at different times, depending on what is happening to us or around us, ranging from being relaxed and uninhibited to feeling more self-conscious. Developing a way of being self-aware (but not uncomfortably self-conscious) seems to be an important step towards managing yourself and your emotions, and it is essential that we communicate this to our children.

I have always talked with my children about the way in which they like to be treated and I remind them that I expect them to use this as a benchmark for their own behaviour. Communication with your child about how she is feeling and what she wants or needs is crucial because it helps us understand how her feelings are linked to certain behaviours.

Such conversations with children need to happen very early on in their lives, and by doing so you can often fend off some behavioural problems before they escalate and sometimes even before they begin.

Children may feel quite self-conscious in a social setting and they might need some tips as to how to become part of a group or pair up with another child. So suggest to your child some ways of starting a game, or encourage her to invite another child over to play. Inviting other children round for a play date can be a very good way of helping your child to develop her social skills. When her friends arrive, stick around and make suggestions for what they could do or play if they seem to be struggling, and make positive comments about how well they are playing together if the atmosphere seems to be happy and harmonious.

Try to play with your child at home whenever possible and if you are playing a competitive game, don't feel that you have to teach her how to lose. In my experience, up to the age of about seven or eight years old, children really find it hard to lose and can become despondent and a bit resentful if they don't win. So instead give her opportunities to win so that you can build up her self-confidence – there will be plenty of opportunities in a number of different arenas later in life in which she can learn to lose!

As parents we have a responsibility to be good role models to our children through our own behaviour, but also to help our children to develop a reflective part of themselves, such as the ability to put themselves in the position of others so they can think about how something feels or appears from the other person's perspective (see Chapter 1).

Turn negatives into positives

Try to think of the difficult times in life as having the potential to be positive experiences; they can provide learning opportunities for both parent and child to help them to establish some of the rules about how we all get along. Ultimately this will teach us the values by which we can all live together more harmoniously.

When children can't get on

How lovely it would be if our children did not fight. But in the real world this is rarely the case. Fighting at some level – amongst siblings or with other children – is a common issue and one that can often leave parents feeling embarrassed (in situations where other people's children are involved), deeply unhappy and, inevitably, worn down by their own efforts to try to keep the peace. It is, sadly, also the case that when fighting breaks out many of these parents will tend to see themselves as failures.

Ultimately, parents wish for their children to get along and to be happy together, but they will find that there are times when the relationship between them breaks down and getting along seems to be impossible. At this point it is really important to try to take a step back from the situation and ask yourself, 'Why now?' Try to work out what has led to this behaviour, what you think might have caused it to erupt and what will happen as a result. Think, too, about whether there is anything that you have done that might have contributed to the situation, and also consider how you are responding to it.

Some of the most common reasons for fighting are down to wanting to get attention or because the children have no other way of solving their problems. How you respond is key to how a child will learn to manage this part of his behaviour and possibly prevent it happening when similar situations arise in the future.

Step back or step in?

Remember, children will fight. This is part of how they work out how to get along with each other and what will be tolerated by their peers. As a parent you have to allow certain fights to run their course (while making sure they don't get out of hand or become physically violent), particularly with issues such as squabbling, because you need to see whether your children are able to resolve these disputes. So keep calm, keep out of the way and ignore the fight if you know that they are not physically hurting each other. However, do step in if you think the dispute has become physical.

Treat both parties similarly as you try to resolve the situation. If you do need to get involved, steer away from simply getting the story about what happened and get them to focus on how they will resolve the situation and do things differently next time. Simply getting an account of events means there'll probably be another argument about who is right!

In any argument or fight, beware of taking sides. It can be very difficult when trying to sort out a dispute, either between siblings or your own child and a friend they have fallen out with, and listening to each side of the story can make the situation feel more complicated. Set out your expectations and thoughts to squabbling children quickly, and tell them that you do not expect them to fight and that fighting, no matter who started it, is not on. Stay impartial and comment on how they might work towards finding a solution. If you get anywhere near someone apologizing, tell him how pleased you are that he is able to appreciate that the other person is upset and leave him with the message that you feel confident he can move on and learn from the experience of falling out.

In terms of enforcing consequences or punishment after a fight, it is easiest to punish both parties involved, otherwise you can get left in the rather peculiar twilight zone of decision-making where you cannot be sure that you have really made the right decision. By punishing both children, this lets them know that you will not take sides, simply because you believe that what they both did was wrong. This also has the added benefit of being a remarkable way of stopping children from telling unnecessary tales, as there is a clear communication that by doing so they will both receive a consequence.

Clearly your aim as a parent is to head off battles before they begin. Watch out for battles as they start to take shape. If you get the sense that a physical altercation is about to ensue this is the time to step in and try to defuse the situation – either by distracting them or by offering them an alternative. You may even want to say out loud that you can see that there is going to be an argument and that you are here to help if they feel they cannot work it out themselves. Just by stating what you see you can take the heat out of a tricky situation, and then all involved will be cued in to paying more attention to their behaviour.

A number of common problems accompany fighting and squabbling. Often children as young as three struggle to manage their anger, particularly when they feel they have been wronged. If a child hasn't been given the clear message by his parents that aggression is not the way to deal with these feelings, he will not know that his response is unacceptable. Help your child to stop reacting in this way by carefully monitoring his responses and intercepting when you feel that he is getting angry. By starting to respond in this way to your child when he is this young, you will be saving yourself some trouble later when he is bigger and less easy to pick up and take away from a confrontation.

Inability to share

The issue of sharing is often problematic. Sharing does not come naturally; it is something that needs to be learnt and cannot be forced (even some adults can find this difficult!).

Young children really have no concept of sharing: birthdays and special occasions are often littered with treats that come in the form of presents, and when a child is given a gift her parents and grandparents tend to say, 'I've bought this especially for YOU.' This statement indicates clearly who the present is for, and therein are the key words: FOR YOU. What would you take from this phrase? A child, quite rightly, will believe that this means that the present is for her, and therefore that it is exclusively hers. No wonder then that problems arise when it comes to sharing. How confusing!

Around the age of two or three years, children begin to reveal an understanding of the fact that there are differences between what a group owns and what is exclusively theirs. This is the time when children begin to say things like 'mine' and 'no', suggesting that they are starting to appreciate that some things, in their mind at least, are their property.

So, unsurprisingly, a child will express her frustration when she is asked to share, especially if she feels that something has been taken away from her before she has had a chance to play with it and satisfy her own needs. I have noticed this with my own children, whereas if they have been allowed time to play with a new toy they have invariably felt much more comfortable about sharing it later. When I have made the mistake of trying to take something away from them too soon, they have let me know how unhappy they are.

Young children up to the age of about three have problems sharing because they only see that somebody else wants to take something from them that they either think or have been told they own. Children of this age don't understand how rewarding it can be to share; all they see is something leaving their possession and not knowing if it will ever be returned. (They will have even less chance of understanding this if they have not even enjoyed the toy themselves yet.)

Usually by the age of three children begin to share and parents must talk positively about this to them, and let their children express their frustrations when they are asked to share something they have.

It is still important, though, that parents do not force a child to share – the feelings that accompany being forced will hardly convince her that it is a good thing to be doing. I have always tried to speak to my children about how much they enjoy a particular toy or activity and have suggested gently that they might like to show it and share it with their brother or sister or a friend.

Keep special toys special

Introducing the idea of sharing gradually gives you an opportunity to work out how special or meaningful a toy is to your child. If you sense that something really is a very special toy that he cannot share then I think it is reasonable to keep it separate and to give it special status. After all, there are times when I hear myself saying to my children that I do not want them to touch certain things because they belong to me.

Beware of double standards in parenting – especially as children get older and they start to notice whether you practise what you preach!

So, to keep playtime harmonious:

O Act as a role model by sharing with other adults and with your child. Let her know that you are sharing something with someone and that you hope they enjoy it as much as you do. Give it away freely and let your child observe you doing this.

○ When you see your child sharing with others be very quick to praise her and say how proud you are of her. By planting these thoughts in her mind you will be giving her a good feeling about what she is doing.

○ Provide opportunities for your children to practise sharing. Set up different games or activities where they have to take turns. Talk to them about waiting, explain that it will be their turn next and acknowledge that you understand how hard it is to wait. Be very enthusiastic about their efforts and give lots of positive praise about how well they have managed.

○ Think about how to avoid fights over toys, especially if the children seem to need your help to stop them getting angry with each other. I have often rather sneakily removed toys or items that seem to cause a row – just for a few days until the dust settles. It can be a red rag to a bull to have certain toys around that they genuinely cannot share.

As with all behaviour, the teaching and praise that you give your children at an early age will allow them to embed in their minds the idea of sharing, which they will then be able to call on at a later date. Depending on the age of the child you are dealing with, as a parent you should be encouraging her to think about how she might manage situations differently so that she does not get into a physical conflict.

Up to the age of about three years old, unless you have a very aggressive child, intervening and picking your child up is the most helpful way of stopping a physical conflict before it takes hold. You must clearly say something like 'no hitting', so that she will begin to associate being removed with the offending behaviour.

From the age of about three you can begin to clearly tell your child that she must not hit other children and that you will prevent her from doing this and you will use time out to help her to learn to stop (see Chapter 3). When children get to about five years of age parents should help by planning ahead and anticipating any potential flashpoints. Often a parent will know which friends trigger an aggressive response, so it might be helpful to point out to your child that she should come to you if she feels that she cannot control her feelings in order that you can step in and help mediate.

One of the things we all forget to do is to notice when our children are getting along well – it can often feel like such

Predict the riot

You might notice that some situations keep ending up in disaster, so these are the ones you need to stage-manage in order to avoid revisiting the same problems. It is reasonable that children may want to keep some toys to themselves, and if this is the case then some forward planning and the removal of that toy before a friend comes around is essential. Also, if particular toys lead to a fracas at home amongst brothers and sisters be clear about when and where they are used.

a relief to have peace and quiet! So put up a big poster to remind yourself that this is the time to say something positive to your children that will acknowledge that you have noticed how well they are all getting along. You want your children to know that you appreciate it when they play well together: children love this sort of attention as it helps them feel noticed, and appreciated, and it helps them to learn what it feels like to have your approval.

Arguing

Children will argue – with their parents, with their brothers and sisters, and with their friends; this is how they try to find ways to negotiate in the world. This process is difficult and painful for both the child and the people around him, and it is important to bear this in mind, otherwise when he begins to argue it can feel like your own child has been kidnapped and a different person has moved into your home.

Children will often attempt to pull the adults around them into an argument, thereby receiving lots of attention. No matter what the age of your child, getting a parent's attention is the key factor driving this behaviour. A fight amongst siblings is guaranteed to provoke parents, so think before you do any-thing. If there is no sign of things getting out of control – and by that I mean individuals getting hurt physically – then there is usually no need to get involved.

By standing back you will be allowing your children the space to try to sort things out for themselves. You need to be around to watch to see that they can solve disagreements without having to argue or for it to develop into a fight. As children begin to settle their conflicts themselves it is important to notice and comment on this, thereby letting them know how pleased you are to see them behaving in this way.

So, to keep arguments under control:

- Do not allow yourself to be pulled into your children's arguments and be careful when you find yourself confronted by this behaviour.

- Remember that arguing can become a bit of a routine: individuals can start to believe that this is the only way to solve conflicts, so if you find yourself in this situation, break the habit and be ready to point out to your child that you can see what is happening and that you would like him to approach the situation differently. Perhaps you both need to sit down or to defer talking about an issue until everyone has the time to do it properly and you are all feeling a bit calmer.

- Hold your line. As a parent I would expect you to say things once and not to be pulled into an argument. Inform your child of your position in the debate and stick to it.

- Remove yourself from a conversation that might become argumentative. This may sound like you are being asked to back down, but I see it more as a way of protecting yourself and your children from getting caught up in a situation that can be avoided and delayed until you are both ready to deal with it. Perhaps you could suggest that the child takes himself off in order to give himself some thinking time.

When the time is right to try to resolve an issue, whether between you and your child or between children, try to play by certain rules. Play down points such as who wins and who loses; what you are hoping for is that both sides feel a reasonable solution has been reached and can live by the outcome. If this can't be agreed on then you will need to discuss it between you, or with them, until there is some acceptance.

Obviously there will be times when your child will not reach an agreement, and if the argument is with you, that will be the point at which you need to remind him that continuing to argue will have a consequence attached. This will give him a clear signal about what will and will not be tolerated.

If the dispute is with another child then you have the authority to say that the disagreement means that something has to come to an end, for example, if they cannot agree they must find something else to do either together or separately. I try not to make my own child back down, but rather treat the situation as if it were a squabble between my children. I do not, however, get into consequences such as time out for other people's children. I state clearly what the rules are in our house and make it clear that I will be letting his parents know what happened when they come to pick him up. These are the expectations that I would have if my children behaved inappropriately in someone else's house and I think parents are usually big enough to listen.

How you behave as a parent informs children of the rules of the household. It would be fabulous if we were all in control all of the time – this is what we aim for – but inevitably there will be lapses. If you resort to screaming and shouting then it should not surprise you if your children do the same, so make sure that they see you settle disputes in a thoughtful and measured way, and show them that this can be done through compromise.

Telling tales

All children tell tales at one time or another. I have come to think about this as a bit of a test: they are trying to find out how much the adult cares about them and are able to protect them.

Most of us can remember very clearly the feeling of being wronged and not being able to do anything there and then, so instead we looked for someone to help us who we believed did have the authority to do something. So cast your mind back and try to remember, what was the result? It might not have been the same for everyone, but I'm sure the majority of you remember being told by the adult not to tell tales. As a parent you now know that you have to respond in this way, otherwise the message is: tell tales and the adults will take your side. As a child I can remember thinking that adults were really unhelpful, but it did stop me from telling tales.

Now I am a parent I have experienced my own children 'telling tales'. When I have been at my best I have remembered to give a lot of acknowledgement to their distress but have said little about what I thought we should do to the offender, and this has often been enough to stop the situation

escalating. At my worst I have become heavily allied with my child and fallen into the 'blame game', which can often cloud a parent's judgement. Questions such as 'what happened?' have not got me very far and have only served to stop the situation being resolved.

So, the most effective way of dealing with children telling tales is:

● Talk to the child about how hard it can be when we feel people are being mean to us and offer her emotional/physical comfort.

● If there are no signs of physical injuries to your child, don't probe the situation any further, instead help her to let the situation go.

● Offer yourself as a sounding board when children feel that they are in a difficult situation. Reframe the conversation and encourage your child to bring an issue to you that she would like some help with. For example, children who share a room are often notorious for telling tales about who made the mess and who wouldn't tidy up, so if your child comes to you with this complaint, get her to think about what she can do so that she feels she is being listened to.

Hitting, kicking and biting

Behaviours such as hitting, kicking and biting are amongst the most problematic for any parent to deal with. Generally I work on the assumption that any behaviour affecting issues such as safety of the person being attacked, or the individual who is attacking, requires the intervention of the adult. By this I mean that a parent needs to stop this behaviour the minute it starts.

Having worked for years with children who display very challenging behaviour, it has been interesting to note that their parents can often recall when it became more tricky to manage their child's behaviour. Clearly this is not the same for everyone, but most often when parents think back they can usually trace this behaviour to when it started. It was most frequently at a time when their child was frustrated and used this behaviour to communicate how upset he was about something.

As with other situations, the key to solving this problem is to unpick the details. Parents will say that they noticed the change, but not how quickly it took hold, while their child realized that behaving like this was a quick and easy way to get what he wanted. In most cases parents found themselves knowingly giving in because they wanted a quick fix for the situation.

Of course, we can all get into this way of behaving and responding: as parents we can often feel that a temporary solution is the best result, but then over time we realize that there was no long-term gain to handling it this way, and that it can even make the situation worse.

So, is aggressive behaviour normal? Children find them-selves in a variety of situations where they become very angry, confused and upset, but until they are the age of four or five they often have very few strategies for managing these powerful emotions, apart from letting them out in a rather ad hoc way. I have watched children who have looked quite shocked at the effect of their outbursts, as if they really had no idea about the impact it might have on the other person.

Often the heart of the problem of aggressive behaviour is that the child does not have the necessary skills to express himself and so he resorts to a physical outburst to vent his frustration. This will temporarily rid him of the feeling that he is experiencing, but it doesn't last and so he will most likely have another, bigger outburst because the situation remains unresolved.

So, good ways to avoid and handle your child's aggression are:

- When you are on the receiving end of a physical outburst, tell your child that you are upset by it so that he knows your feelings have been hurt. By doing this you will be teaching him to put himself in your position and to think about what it feels like to be on the receiving end of such aggression.

- Talk to your child and tell him what you think he is feeling. This can help to diffuse a situation – it doesn't always work, but it can give a child a way out. By doing this you are effectively saying that he doesn't need to have the outburst because you know that he is upset; then, by using some emotional language, you offer an alternative, which is to talk about what is bothering him.

- Prevent these explosions happening in the first instance.

As parents we should try to notice the patterns in our children's behaviour, so if we know that a comment or an action is going to result in a right hook it is our job to make sure this trigger is avoided.

○ Teach children to recognize when a situation is becoming aggressive and confrontational and to then take themselves away from it to go and seek out an adult.

Managing aggressive behaviour can be both physically and mentally exhausting, so an abundance of patience is needed. Our children watch our every movement, and if they notice that we really cannot cope with a behaviour then they will continue to use it in order to test us.

Always make it clear to your child that a physical outburst will be responded to with a zero-tolerance approach. With almost all cases you need to walk in and remove the person who is being violent and keep them separate from the other person until they are calm. I would recommend using time out in such situations, as it gives everyone the opportunity to calm down separately rather than suffer the indignity of being held and possibly worsening the problem – which I'm sure no parent would want to do.

Allow your child to calm down completely before you start talking to him about the incident. Do not try to discuss it with your child while he is cooling off, as this will only throw more fuel on the fire and perhaps even cause a re-escalation in his behaviour.

Going forward – enhancing your child's social skills

I hope that from all this you can see that your child needs your help and guidance in negotiating her way over the many hurdles that are ahead of her.

What drives difficult or 'naughty' behaviour in children is the desire to gain the attention of adults, so if you can give your child more positive attention I can guarantee you will find that many of these behaviours decrease. Just spending a small amount of time with your child each day can reduce her need to seek out your attention in less desirable ways. (See Chapter 2 on how to make time for your children.)

Even spending ten minutes a day with your child can have a big impact on her behaviour. When I have discussed this with parents they often say, 'But we do play with our child every day, and we do give her special time.' This might well be true in their minds, but I'm not talking about activities that are academically led, or starting an activity with her and then sitting back to watch a television programme or make a cup of tea. I'm talking about concentrated time. This means no making tea, no taking phone calls, just sitting with your child and allowing yourself to be led by her.

Ask her what she would like to do and how you can join in. If it is clear that she just wants you to watch her doing whatever it is she is doing, do so and make positive comments about what you see. Just this simple act will make her feel very special and, in turn, will enhance her self-confidence.

It also teaches children about being appreciated, and these feelings are important because they provide a good starting point where children can feel positive about the contribution they make to a situation.

Organize activities at home which involve all of your children playing a game or doing a craft-type activity. You will have to work hard at noticing what your children are doing and comment on this. You also need to say clearly how well you think that they are all working together to help them to appreciate the idea of cooperation and the pleasure that it can bring to them and to you.

Use the opportunities of having friends, family or other visitors over to extend your child's social skills in different situations. Before the visitors arrive, set out your expectations to your child of how she should behave. Be clear that there will be consequences for both good and difficult behaviour. If you find that situations keep arising that are awkward and troublesome, then stage manage them so that you can see where confrontations begin. By doing this you will be able to help your child find ways of getting along that are successful.

Don't take play arrangements for granted until you are happy about how all the children will behave. Always make yourself available – either in the same room or in the room next door. This might sound a bit extreme, but I think it is important in helping children to understand that you do care about how they get along. Of course, on the upside, it also means that you are on hand to give hearty praise to everyone for having fun together. You know your own child and therefore when you think they are ready for this kind of activity, but I believe that, generally, when children begin attending school they are usually ready to be left for longer periods at a friend's house.

Don't forget

O Encourage your children to treat others as they would like to be treated.

O Expect your children to argue and fight – they need to practise how to resolve disputes.

O Don't get involved in an argument unless your children are being physically aggressive towards each other or the situation starts to get out of hand.

O Remove children from an antagonistic situation and use consequences such as time out (for your own children) if they display excessively aggressive physical behaviour.

O Sharing does not come naturally to children.

O Always consider the developmental stage that your child is at – she will need to learn how to express any feelings of anger and frustration in ways that are socially acceptable.

Say 'no' to rudeness and swearing

Swearing and generally being rude can cause parents and children all sorts of problems. In the home and outside of it the language that your child uses is vitally important, because it provides a very quick gauge for others to assess what you as a parent feel is acceptable language for your child to be using.

If your children are polite and use appropriate language then you are deemed to be in a winning situation, as people will comment on how well-mannered and well-spoken your child is. If, however, your child is rude then a completely different picture emerges and parents will be judged for not taking a firm stand and addressing this issue head on.

So where are they getting this from?

It can throw us completely, or overwhelm us, when our children start using words that we don't want them to use. As soon as a child begins to use inappropriate language you need to find out where the words are coming from and why they have been adopted. Children encounter many different environments from day to day which will impact on them, but in my experience it does not take too long to track down the source for this new vocabulary.

It is terribly important also to consider why children begin to use language in this way, because knowing this will help you to stop them doing it. It might start for a number of reasons, including:

- Exposure to this language in the different environments they are in, for example, home, school, social settings.
- As a way of expressing anger.
- As a way of expressing frustration.
- They get a response and attention for using rude words.

The different environments that children inhabit give them so much information: about how we behave when we are together, what is acceptable and also about the way in which we speak to each other. If your child is growing up in a household where swearing is used freely then you shouldn't be surprised to hear him swearing, either in front of his friends or before you. Having said this, I still find that parents do not always see the connection between the language they are using and what comes out of their own child's mouth; it is as if parents expect their child to have a way of filtering the language he hears so that he only tunes into the good bits.

In a child's quest to learn he is absorbing absolutely everything that goes on around him. Not all these lessons happen at home, and children will be exposed to swearing in a variety of other situations – school is often the most likely place where rude words will be explored and shared. Children will quickly begin to understand that this language is wrong and that it has a tremendous impact when used. We all know that children definitely pick and choose when to use offensive language, which in itself shows that they know it is wrong. They will pick up this message from adults – how often have you seen an adult mouth a swear word or even put his hand over his lips quickly when the odd word slips out? Most adults know that they shouldn't do these things, and so for this reason it is vital that you curb your language in front of your child and make this a new habit when you have children. A young baby cannot speak, but it is worth training yourself to stop swearing before you get to the stage where he will pick up on it and repeat what you have said.

So, if you want to nip this problem in the bud:

O Make sure your child understands that you expect him to use language in a respectful way.

O Comment positively on the language your child uses, particularly if you know that the language his friends use is unpleasant.

O Think about your own language – is it really necessary to swear? Stop using bad language while your children are young and they will not pick it up. Get other adults to help you spot the times when you swear – you may be surprised at how many times you slip up.

Tackling bad language

Children need to be taught from a very young age that language is a powerful tool, which can have considerable impact when used in both positive and negative ways, and that they need to take other people's thoughts and feelings into consideration before they say things.

As parents we should all have high expectations on this matter, and our children need to know that we want them to conduct themselves in a certain way. These expectations will equip children to get along in society in a way that is respectful and shows an awareness of other people's feelings.

If, or when, language that is offensive or inappropriate does appear, parents have to be quick to act, and so this is an area you need to plan for, just in case the situation should arise. First, try to identify what needs to be tackled in your household, in terms of the language that is being used, then deal with it according to the problem (see below for solutions to specific issues).

The different social situations you expose your child to can be occasions where swearing 'slips' out, or is just present, and your child will pick up on what is being said. Children will be watching to see how adults respond when bad language is used, so if swearing is accompanied by a lot of laughing and joking then they receive the message that this is something that is fine and even quite amusing. If adults look embarrassed or get rather cross though, a child will assume that this language is an acceptable short cut for letting people know they are not in the best of moods.

Either way, if the general feeling is that it is OK to use this language to communicate then we cannot be surprised to hear children pop these words into their own conversation. So:

○ Treat swearing seriously; tell your child clearly that you do not expect her to use bad language.

○ If you swear, expect that your child will develop this habit. Take responsibility for this behaviour and don't blame other people for it.

○ When children reach around ten years of age ask them what they think the words they are using mean and then, if you feel it is appropriate, let them know how offensive some of these words are.

Swearing in anger

Expressing anger through swearing is very common: situations that adults find difficult to manage – whether on the telephone, at the shops or in the car – are often those where swearing is most widely used. The lesson for a child here is quite straightforward: when things get too much and you feel like you may lose control, insert a swear word.

Using swearing in this way teaches our children very limited ways of dealing with their anger. A swear word may provide some temporary relief, but I am not convinced that it really makes angry feelings disappear. We have to show our children that as adults we can deal with these sorts of thoughts and feelings and won't let them spill over into swearing. We all get upset and angry at times, but the most powerful way of dealing with this is to recognize what is happening, to give ourselves some cooling off time and then to talk to someone about what is making us feel this way.

Perhaps an area that is often not tackled explicitly is when swearing is used to express feelings of aggression and violence verbally rather than physically. In some families where tensions run high and can spill over into violence, swearing can act as a precursor and can be a useful warning that the situation is becoming dangerous.

Children in this situation may use this language as a cue to disappear, or they may use this style of communication themselves. Either way, parents owe it to their children to think about what happens when swearing is used and not pretend that it is just something that happens in their family, without giving it the thought and attention it deserves.

In families where there is a high level of aggression, there are often very real and different problems because these families find it impossible to see what is happening around them and to understand the intensely difficult feelings they are surrounded by. A child living in this environment will inevitably experience significant difficulties in developing healthy ways of relating to others.

So set high standards at home and insist that your child finds alternative ways to express strong feelings. Encourage him to talk about his frustrations and make sure that you give him the time he needs for you to help him with this. Ask him how he is feeling and why he thinks he became so cross. Finally, consider how swearing is being used in your home. Is bad language being used to stop adults becoming physically violent? If so, there is a problem and you should seek help from someone like your GP so that you can get to the bottom of these feelings and find out where they are coming from.

Swearing and frustration

Think about how many times you have used, or have been tempted to use, swear words because you are frustrated. If you have sworn then you probably think you were quite discreet and that your child won't have noticed; but you'd be wrong. Often children are on hand to hear you; they might not hear the actual word, but they will probably realize you are saying something which indicates you are cross or frustrated. I have sat in many sessions where parents have been enlightened by their children who can very accurately tell me what words the adults use when they are cross or frustrated.

Another factor as to why children use bad language in this way is the amount of language that a child has at her disposal. Children who find it difficult to express themselves and have a tendency to lose control can often rely on swearing as a way of making their feelings known. So if a child sees swearing as a quick way of communicating their frustration, she can start to use it when she has these feelings herself.

Many of the children I meet in my work use swearing as a sort of shorthand for expressing an emotion they find difficult to describe or talk about. So if your child is struggling to find the words to express her frustrations, help her to find another way to do so and encourage her to use statements such as 'I feel...' or 'I think...' instead.

Swearing for effect

Perhaps the most popular reason why children swear is because of the guaranteed attention it will receive from their parents or other people around them. A swearing child is probably one of the biggest crowd-stoppers and can cause huge embarrassment to most parents – not least because it allows other people to make sweeping judgements about what standards parents have set.

So if a child does get a response when using bad language he might well continue to speak this way for just this reason. Many of us can recall a time when adults have been sitting together and suddenly you hear a little voice utter a rude word. Before the adults have time to take this in there is usually a stunned silence. This silence reveals your first response – that this is wrong – and this is the response I would urge all parents to hold on to. It feels wrong, because it is wrong. So stop and think before you respond to your child's swearing; by ignoring the language and not reacting to it he will be forced to find other ways to get your attention.

If you have older children you might witness the pressure from friends that can make children feel they need to copy them and speak the same way, so help your child to make his own choices. Hopefully the standards that you set at home will also help give him the confidence not to fall into bad habits. In the same vein, encourage your child to see that swearing is not cool but that it makes people form more general negative opinions about him. With older children (aged ten and above)

ask them how they would like to be viewed by the family and the general public, and explain that it will be difficult for adults to have a positive view if they are heard swearing.

Stamp out bad language

For me, swearing is a zero-tolerance zone! Swearing in young children simply sounds appalling. I am often left feeling very shocked and irritated that children resort to swearing as a means of communication.

Speak up on swearing

I believe that children should be encouraged to use language to express themselves with the proviso that they can get their point across without offending others. In my view, swearing is a shorthand approach to speaking; I have confronted many children in a very open-handed way by saying that I do not expect to hear them swearing or to be spoken to in this way. Surprisingly, this has usually been enough to stop them and often the children have apologized, thought carefully about their language and started to use less offensive words.

What is interesting to see, though, is how much help children need to express their thoughts, and understanding this has made me realize why using this short cut is so appealing to them in the first place.

One good solution to this problem is to provide children with a different vocabulary that does not include swear words. Introducing alternative words which are slightly silly can be helpful to some children, because they act as a reminder to parents and children alike that they need to be more vigilant when speaking to each other because bad language is not acceptable. Words such as 'sunshine' and 'sunflowers' are good ones that many people can agree on and use, and when they substitute them, many families are suddenly aware of how many swear words they were actually using!

Often children rely on the impact that swear words have without really knowing what they mean, so if your child is using lots of swear words, or one in particular, ask her to tell you what she thinks they mean. Explain to her that the words she is saying are very rude and are hurtful. This discussion has another purpose, too, in that understanding what your child is trying to demonstrate through this language will give you an idea about what emotions she is attempting to express. Armed with this information you will be able to help her find the right words to describe the feelings she is experiencing, which might in turn bring a natural end to her use of swear words for that purpose.

Swearing has to remain high on your radar and you have to find creative ways to break the cycle. If swearing persists after you have discussed the whys and wherefores of it with your child, you may find that she responds better to a programme of incentives such as a sticker chart.

Set the standard at home

Of course, not all bad language comes from the parents' example at home; you should also consider the limits that you set in your child's environment. For example, there are restrictions placed on television programmes and films and you have some control over these. If you do not exert your parental authority here you leave the door open for your child to find his way to these words in a rather unregulated way.

The television and film industry does put some limits in place to protect children from inappropriate language and behaviour, but children will talk about what they have watched in other settings, such as in class and in the playground. Television programmes and films can glamorize swearing: it can look harmless, but if this is the impression that children also receive they will begin to incorporate these words into their own language.

So you need to set the standard. Keep an eye on what your child is being exposed to at home, and even at other children's houses. If you are not happy with what he is watching at home, or elsewhere, it is up to you to say and do something about it.

Depending on the frequency of your child's swearing, break up the day into sections and give awards for each section where swear words are not used. These awards have to be linked to rewards, which should be something like choosing activities that can be done together at home – such as playing board games, reading together, watching videos, and so on. These sorts of rewards are far more valuable than buying treats that they might get anyway, and rewarding a child in this way also reinforces the fact that you want to be with her and that you value your time with her.

So, to stamp out bad language:

○ Make it clear that you will not tolerate swearing and that there will be consequences for using bad language.

○ Remember that children often need a lot of help to find the words they need to explain how they are feeling.

○ If swearing persists, provide your child with different words that are silly and non-offensive.

○ Do not rise to bad language initially; use the tactic of ignoring and see where this takes you. You only need to act if not reacting is not effective.

○ Do not sit back and accept the language your children bring home.

Be responsible for what your children watch on the television, who they are mixing with and also the language that they are being exposed to. Again, if you hear your child repeating bad language, make it clear to her immediately that you do not want to hear this language from her.

Stop the swearing around your child

As adults we often find ourselves in situations where there is a lot of swearing. It can be very easy to fall into the trap of thinking that this is just a bit of fun and to switch off from it, but if that's true, why does it feel so uncomfortable?

Think about the situations you find yourself in and how comfortable you find them, and don't be afraid to say if you would like someone to change their language. It can be difficult and possibly awkward, but if we are expecting our children not to swear we have to pay attention to our own behaviour and sometimes that of others around us.

A much easier situation to control is when adult friends swear in front of your children. Be quick to pick up on this and don't be embarrassed to ask them not to use this language.

Name-calling

This is an area of behaviour that can seem fairly harmless, but it forces us to think very carefully about what is being communicated. Name-calling can range from using words such as sissy, idiot, fool, chump, and so on, to far more offensive words that insult a person's culture, size or unusual features.

The nature of name-calling is two-fold: it seems to me that it can be designed to insult the other person, but it can also be used as a term of endearment.

If the person who is doing the name-calling is uttering the word to offend then you need to question what drives him to insult or hurt someone in this way and what is stopping him from talking things through with someone. Clearly this behaviour is his way of getting a message across very quickly and with maximum impact.

Name-calling is usually not intended to hurt, but is used more as a term of affection. This is quite a complex situation, and if you hear your child doing this you need to explain to him that calling another child a name has to be thought about carefully, particularly if the word being used has some accuracy within it. If not checked out, these sort of comments can be more harmful than they were intended to be, and in the long term they can gradually chip away at an individual's self-confidence, making him feel very vulnerable.

If there is any doubt about the function of name-calling, consider how children sometimes speak to themselves when they have done something wrong. I have heard my children calling themselves names which are clearly a put-down. Even if it is said in jest, it is horrible to hear and leaves me worried about how they view themselves.

I'm not sure that there are ever any really acceptable names. I say this because often adults will say that they were hurt by the names but, because they seemed to be said in jest, they did not want to make a fuss. Ultimately name-calling can get us into tricky waters, so it's often better not to do it at all. However, we need to explain to our children that if a name does slip out then they ought to think about why they said what they did and to decide quickly on a way to repair the damage it might have caused. So,

O Accept that name-calling is not acceptable – it is often experienced as being extremely hurtful, even if it is said in jest.

O Remember that all language is open to interpretation; if there is a chance that it could be taken the wrong way then it's best to steer clear.

Nipping name-calling in the bud

You need to be firm with your child about what constitutes acceptable and unacceptable naming of other people. If children grow up with confusion about what name-calling really means then it can lead to all sorts of problems, particularly if they start to do it at school. I have heard children saying they did not mean to cause offence, but if you ask the recipient what she believes you'll find she is not always so convinced.

Talk with your child about what she actually means when she calls another person a name and see if you can establish what it is she is trying to say. Having empathy for another person is a skill, which children need to work on. It is always helpful to ask a child how she would feel if she was called a name and how she thinks she might react to it; often a rather defensive response such as 'I wouldn't mind' or 'I know it would be a joke' or 'I wouldn't care' can form the basis for a really rich conversation about how someone else might feel. Asking a child why she thinks someone else might feel differently to her is key to getting her to put herself in someone else's shoes. It can be very easy to try to take the line of 'I didn't mean it to be hurtful', but if a comment is taken negatively then the name caller has to take responsibility for making the other person feel upset or uncomfortable.

With children aged five and above it can be helpful to introduce the idea of reparation. Reparation is an important part of helping your child understand the impact her behaviour has had on someone else and the need to repair this. It is a good idea to put both children together and ask them to talk about what happened to get a sense of how the child who was at the receiving end of the name calling felt.

Step in before it starts

I have always (both at home and in my work) stressed to children from an early age that they should use kind words to each other. This isn't always successful, but it helps a child take responsibility for his behaviour. If a child later uses hurtful words or phrases, adults are in a better position to challenge him, as they know he has been asked to use different words.

With a much younger child you should get in early and anticipate frustration and anger if this tends to lead to him using bad language. Quickly say that you can see that he is becoming upset or that he is finding something difficult and provide a space for this to be discussed.

This skill takes time to perfect, but it can really help a child negotiate a way through to say sorry and to recognize the hurt she has caused. It also teaches the person who has been upset that she has the right to stand up for herself, be heard and not suffer in silence. It does require quite phenomenal refereeing qualities and great patience on the adult's part, but in my opinion it pays dividends in the long run as children begin to develop their own skills to reflect on their behaviour.

Saying things that upset others

This is another form of language that is very unhelpful. Children who say things to upset others on a regular basis often do it because they have understood the impact their comments have on others. So, remarking on somebody's ability to do things or just making a comment that is uncalled for needs to be clamped down on immediately.

In my experience children tend to make comments like this to deflect attention from how they are feeling, and so this is another area of behaviour where a child needs to be taken to task about what he is doing. You need to tell him that he cannot say nasty things to people as a way of relieving his own anger, and instead he should find another, less hurtful way of letting others know that he is upset with them. Explain to your child that just saying something to upset another person is a cowardly way of dealing with what might be a very important communication. Help your child to think about what has upset him and what it is he wants to say to the other person. Encourage him to speak to the other person with an adult present to help him describe his feelings and thoughts in a respectful way.

Try to head off this behaviour before it begins; encourage your child to think about and work out what it is he really wants to say before he speaks. Look for the meaning behind a comment – there are some who believe there is no such thing as a throwaway comment, and I am inclined to agree with them. If you think about the things people have said that have upset you, I'm sure that one of the reasons you were upset was because of the meaning you gave to their words.

This is the message we need to get across to our children, and, again, their ability to empathize with others is key.

Set the standards for language at home

Once more, how you behave in front of your children is crucial to getting polite, sociable behaviour from them. To be a good role model swearing, name-calling and saying upsetting things should be steered clear of.

Hand on heart, it would be difficult to say that I had never been guilty of doing these things but, thankfully, it made me feel so bad afterwards that it served as a reminder of how awful behaving like this can be for others and also for yourself.

Look at your own behaviour

We all make mistakes, and by admitting to our children that we are aware we have done something wrong, we can each learn from this. It provides a helpful standpoint, which allows them to know that they can, and will, make mistakes and that it's OK to do so.

Make a point of insisting on polite, kind language at home and you will find that children rise to these expectations and will talk openly about any rude language they encounter. My view is that swearing should be banned at home and that adults have to be vigilant and point out to each other when there is slippage. It is especially important to apologize for any

Sarcastic? Me?

It can be tempting to use sarcasm to deal with difficult situations, because in many ways it makes a telling off seem less harsh. However what actually happens is that there is a very unclear communication and children are left unsure if they have done something wrong.

Sarcasm can be a rather backhanded way of letting someone know what you really think of them. This is often too subtle for a young child to understand and can just make her feel guilty, bad or ashamed. So stick to straightforward reprimands and make it clear to her what it is you object to about her behaviour. Being upfront leads to far quicker results.

bad language spoken in front of children, as this allows a child to see that adults are conscious of behaving appropriately.

In addition, try to explain to your child why you or another adult spoke in this way. Let her know that sometimes words are used when people become frustrated, but that it is not a good or acceptable way of expressing yourself.

What if swearing and rudeness are combined with tantrums?

The combination of these two behaviours can really push parents' limits. When challenged in this way I have always tried to think about which behaviour I want to stop as a priority. Given these issues, I would deal with the tantrums first.

Target this behaviour in the usual way – by using the techniques of ignoring and time out – and initially do not respond to the language issue, because you can't deal with everything at once. I would be explicit about what you are doing and tell your child about the tactic you are using. Say clearly to him, 'I am ignoring what you are saying.'

With time, and a lot of patience, you may get to the point where you have the tantrums under control and you are able to target the swearing more directly.

So, then follow these stages:

O Ask your child what he is trying to tell you when he uses these words.

○ Talk to your child about what these words mean.

○ With persistent offenders, offer the alternative silly words that may help him to break the pattern and help him to realize how often he swears.

○ With older children, set up incentives for stopping by giving them a pile of counters which are equivalent to an amount of money. Each time your child swears take a counter/coin away. Decide on the frequency of this to help you tailor the programme to his needs.

○ Develop your own awareness around your own language and cut back on your personal use of expletives.

How you hold yourself together is crucial to any intervention where you hope to have a positive impact on your child's behaviour, so don't rant and rave or swear at him. Don't panic either: tell yourself that this is something you can tackle. If you start to lose faith enlist the help of others, and don't let friends and family swear in your child's presence.

When you start to win the battle, don't take progress for granted. Acknowledge and celebrate the success with your child so that he can see how important this achievement is for both of you. Do not for a minute think that he will just grow out of it: this passive response will only make the situation worse.

Help your children to express themselves more effectively

Ultimately you want to shape your child's behaviour in order that she becomes an individual who can express herself in a sensitive and respectful way that shows she understands the impact of her words. In order to achieve this, it is important to set up opportunities for her to develop these skills in a range of situations.

From a very early age the way that you speak to your child has an impact, so try to pay attention to the different tones that you use and the manner in which you speak. Children become very confused if parents give them mixed messages about what we as adults are allowed to do, particularly if this differs dramatically from our expectations of them.

Decide on a code of conduct; this probably sounds rather serious, but it is helpful to think about what language you will tolerate in your home. If you live in a household where adults swear and call each other names, whether in anger or in jest, this will have an impact on your child.

Try not to overreact if your children start to talk in a way that you do not like; remember that they are learning about what is acceptable and what is not, and it is your job as a parent to help them find the right way to communicate.

For young children under five who perhaps struggle to find ways to express their emotions in an appropriate way, try to pre-empt the situation by describing how you think they are feeling. This shows them that you are not trying to ignore their feelings but are helping them tell you what it is about. Help them by breaking down their account into more manageable chunks. This can be incredibly affirming for a young child and helps her develop a sense that you are interested and want to help.

With slightly older children I think it is important not to labour the point when you hear inappropriate words. Rather you should say very firmly that you do not like those words and suggest others that they might use instead to describe their thoughts and feelings. Alongside this gentle reminder, and depending on the age of your child, I would suggest you begin to talk with her about the words she is using and discuss the impact of these words. Some children simply have not grasped how off-putting their language is, and knowing this can be enough to stop them.

The richness of the language used by your child will largely come from you and the material you have at home. How you allow her to express her emotional state will be a key factor in how she uses the language that is available to her. Again, you will be a model for this. Bottling things up or just letting them spill out is very confusing because issues will not get resolved in a helpful way. Find a happy balance: let your child know that feeling upset and angry is fine but that it is important to talk about these feelings.

Of course, everyone makes mistakes from time to time and outbursts can happen when a situation becomes out of hand. If this is the case you must acknowledge this is happening and rather than getting angry about it it is often more effective to initiate a discussion about how the person might have behaved differently.

Don't forget

O Children learn from adults, so if you swear then you should expect your child to follow suit.

O Be clear about your expectations and be sure to let your child know that rudeness and swearing will not be tolerated.

O Help your child to develop more effective ways of communicating his frustration or anger; help him to plan what it is he wants to say and help him find the words to do this.

O Do not be drawn in by swearing. Ignoring can often be a good way of showing your child that you are not going to reward/notice this behaviour.

O Think about the impact of name-calling and sarcasm – it can seem like a joke, but at what cost to the person on the receiving end?

O Set yourself the challenge of providing an environment for your child that is full of rich language and where he has help to develop his language skills. In such a situation he will not feel tempted to resort to the short cuts that result in inappropriate and less desirable language.

Managing defiance

The words 'no', 'don't want to' and 'make me' epitomize defiance. From a very early age, young children will test the limits set by a parent, and this is a normal stage in your child's development. At around the age of two, you can expect this defiant behaviour to peak and it will then balance out until it rears its head again in adolescence.

From about two years old, children are learning that people have different wishes, and they are beginning to realize that the choices they make will have an impact on how their parent reacts. In order to test out this discovery, a child will behave in particular trying ways, and common areas of difficulty include:

- Not doing what he is told.
- Avoiding bedtime.
- Running off in the park when called.
- Running off when out generally, for example, at the shops.
- Walking home from school behind everybody.
- Not turning the television or the computer off when asked.
- Not completing homework.

Testing times

This testing behaviour gives a child the opportunity to see what happens when conflict occurs. Even very young children will try certain behaviours to see if parents are surprised at what they are doing and whether they will react to it.

An example that sticks in my mind, because I have seen it happen over and over again, is this: even very young children know that their food is supposed to stay in the bowl in which it is served and that parents do not want to see their child tipping her food over the floor. However, picture the scene as it is played out in many households.

Almost in slow motion, visualize a young child holding her bowl very near to the edge of her high chair ready to let the food tip over the edge. At the point at which she lets go, many children watch very carefully to see how her parent reacts, and this reaction will be her guide for other situations.

Often a child will accompany this type of behaviour with the phrase 'uh oh', which might be her attempt to try to make it look accidental, but both you and your child know that at the moment the bowl begins to fall this situation can lead to potential conflict.

You can probably think of numerous other times when your child did something that you were sure she knew was wrong, almost as a test to see how you would react. Think back to those situations and remember what happened; pay attention during any future ones and compare notes and see if you can get some insight into what is going on. Observing your child's defiant behaviour can give you clues as to what you need to do to head off such situations. Noticing when these behaviours occur and when they don't can help you track the start of a defiant phase and to manage future situations differently and more calmly as and when they arise.

Making a stand

When a child is one to two years old you will hear him practising using words such as 'no' and 'don't want to'. Initially he will try these out on you to see your reaction. Then, depending on your response and as your child learns the power of these words, he will begin to use them in different ways. Often he will do this to try to assert his independence and in an attempt to control different situations.

As your child gets slightly older – probably from the age of around five years and above – you will notice that his behaviour starts to change too. You may notice him deliberately doing the opposite of what you ask, again to test the boundaries you have created. His body language will also change and you may even be treated to the classic standoff position that children often take – putting his hands on his hips with an accompanying sigh – whenever you ask him to do something he doesn't want to do!

From the age of six onwards you will see your child developing selective hearing: you may find yourself calling to him to get his attention, or giving him an instruction, only to find that he does not respond.

Another favourite with all children is the delaying tactic that they use to gain more time; typically you will hear a compliant voice saying 'in a minute' whenever you ask them to do something. This is used most often if you have fallen into the trap of not being specific about what you want done and when. Children will very quickly notice how you ask them to do something, and if you are non-specific about the timescales you want them to work towards you will find yourself inviting this response.

Children aged ten and above will continue to demonstrate their independence and test your authority and will typically flex their defiant muscles as they continue to try to develop their sense of self. At this age it is important for your child to begin to practise his skills of negotiation with you, and this is OK if you can insist that it is done respectfully. However, you might decide to compromise on this a little if it seems appropriate in your situation.

Unfortunately, you might well find from one time to another that you are witnessing your child displaying a combination of all the behaviours above – and this is a very interesting cocktail to have to handle all at the same time.

I have always found that being clear about what I expect is the most effective way of stopping defiant behaviour. Ask your child to do things within a time frame that is reasonable and don't be persuaded to compromise – or this may start him thinking that everything is up for debate. Look at your body language and listen to your tone of voice, and make sure that you are not sending out messages to your defiant child that he is interpreting as a challenge to rise to. Finally, remain calm and don't be thrown off-balance by your child's defiant display. Stick to the initial request you made, otherwise you will find yourself going off at a tangent and your original request may well become lost.

Why is this happening?

It is very important not to feel overly persecuted by your child's defiant behaviour. As a parent it can feel like you are banging your own head against a brick wall, but spending time trying to understand why this behaviour is happening can be a helpful step towards working out what is really going on.

Children often have difficult temperaments, which can result in them instinctively taking up a position that is directly opposed to you and your request. Given that this may be the case, you need to be aware of this and adapt your behaviour accordingly to ensure that you are not responding in a way that feeds into this behaviour.

Think about your family: are different members mostly compliant, or is everything a bit of a battleground? Certainly I know that there can be days when my children are defiant or difficult and, depending on my response to them, this can go either way. The situation can either be headed off fairly successfully or, if I am not being very active in my thinking, I can make the situation much worse by digging my heels in – which ultimately results in everyone being unhappy.

Who's in control?

If you and your family have a tendency to question and make everything difficult, then this is most likely what your child will learn to do too. She will soon realize that there is an opportunity to make people very angry by just saying 'no' and so she will choose not to move from this position.

Your challenging child

Children who are particularly defiant often have a low level of frustration. For whatever reason, these children don't seem to have mastered the skill of holding themselves together in order to manage their frustration when asked to do something. A child who struggles in this way will immediately feel either anger or frustration if, for example, he is asked to tidy his room and he will demonstrate this in different ways, such as a tantrum, shouting, or lots of banging and crashing.

These children need a certain type of handling if you want to prevent head-on battles every time you ask them to do something. Often when parents talk to me about how difficult it is to get their child to do what they ask, we have to sit and unpick the situation. A few common themes will usually emerge.

Children who challenge their parents by refusing to complete the task are often those who require a lot of warning and time to be able to respond to a request. Asking these children to do something immediately feels to them as if you are trying to take away their power. Setting the scene and explaining that you know he doesn't want to do the task can also be really helpful. Just a little acknowledgement allows a child to realize that you are trying to understand his frustration. And finally, having a list of jobs that your child has to complete can often give him the sense that he is more in control, and this in turn can make him feel more able to do what has been asked.

This stance gives your child a huge amount of control and influence over what happens in your home. Perhaps she behaves in this way because she feels there are very few opportunities to feel in control, or perhaps she has observed either parent gaining the upper hand in this way. Or maybe it is just that she has had an experience where being defiant allowed her to get away with things because her parents gave in for a quiet life.

Stand your ground

Here's another classic, tried and tested routine some of you may recognize. Your child might have learned just how long to maintain his defiance and then, at the last minute, he will throw in a tantrum or hurt himself in a way that means his parents feels sorry for him and give him a cuddle.

Unless you track this type of situation carefully you will find yourself forgetting about the job you asked him to do and attending to the immediate behaviour that is in front of you. What your child has learned here is that he can up the intensity of his behaviour in order to avoid doing something he doesn't want to do. So be aware that this might happen and provide comfort, but restate that the request has to be completed within a certain amount of time or there will be a consequence, such as losing time on a favourite game.

Some children enjoy seeing how long they can defy their parents as they like to feel that they are winning the battle. I have worked with children who try to wind me up and literally wait until they have had their fun, seen me get cross and then at the last minute, when they are feeling triumphant, they agree to do what I have asked. This behaviour will leave me regretting that I didn't stick to what I know and not get involved in battles of this sort in the first place.

However, there are also other pay-offs for children when they are being defiant: it can give them the sense that they can do what they want for longer, and that feeling in itself is worth the battle. How many times have you asked your child to put her toys away only to have her stall you either by saying nothing or that she will do it in a minute? When you step back and look at this situation, what do you observe? When I have allowed myself to look back on such a scene I usually see myself working up into a frenzy while my child is sitting having a lovely time!

Children learn how to control us as a result of how we respond to them. This should not come as such a surprise when you think about the behaviour that you as a parent use to control your child. Time and time again I have watched parents ask a child to do something. The request is usually made in a calm way the first and second time; then, after two or more refusals, suddenly the stakes are upped and the parent shouts out their request in order to get a response. The child has learnt that a certain amount of defiance works and will buy

her a little extra time, but when mum loses her temper then it is time to act, because you know that she really means it. Up until then, for some children, it can feel like it's just a game.

I know this is a trap I can fall into, particularly when I am tired. The minute I hear the tone of my voice change I know it's time to rethink my behaviour and what it says to my children. Both parent and child can find ways of using their behaviour to ensure that, in their own mind at least, they win a situation.

When faced with a busy schedule and situations that can easily unravel because you are tired, I have always resorted to having a discussion with my children where we all sit down and try to identify what needs to be done. I find this helpful because it can be so easy to lose track of who is expected to

Who's in control?

The usual issue of how you set up and maintain adult and child boundaries in your household are key when identifying who is in control. In today's society parents talk about not wanting to suppress their child's spirit or individuality, and giving them a voice or treating them as an equal. This is, I'm afraid, the beginning of a situation littered with difficulty because there are inevitably differences in roles and responsibilities that just cannot be fudged. There will always come a point where adults pull rank and assert themselves, even if that had not been their intention.

do what that I have to write things down. After moaning about this constant visual reminder, my children then organize themselves and just get on with what has been asked of them.

How can you stand up to defiance?

As I have repeated throughout this book, if a parent has high expectations and standards it will help a child to know what is expected of him. If you are inconsistent with these expectations he will learn that there is a certain percentage of time when he does not need to listen or take notice of requests that you might make of him.

Think about yourself and your current, or your last, work placement. If your boss never made it clear that you had to be at work at a certain time you would have no motivation to be punctual, but if you had a boss who noticed just some of the time the likelihood is that you would try to get in at a traditional start time. However, if your boss had high expectations and clearly stated what time he expected you in, I'm sure you would always make your best effort to start at the expected time.

Bearing this scenario in mind, think about the different expectations you have of your child and then think about the areas of conflict that arise around them – I know there are many grey areas around my expectations that would benefit from more clarity.

Give your child fair warning

I support parents who have high expectations of their children and who expect them to do what they are told. However, I do think that all children need to be given some take up time. By this I mean that they benefit from opportunities to think about leaving whatever they are doing before they do as they have been asked. Be reasonable; don't expect them to jump up straight away when you ask them to do something. If you want them to lay the table don't ask them to do it when you have already served the food; ask 20 minutes before you are ready, then you know that you have time to give prompts.

So, for example, let's think about a morning routine with your children. Your list of things to do might include:

O Wake up when called.

O Get dressed before having breakfast.

O Brush teeth after breakfast.

O No watching the television before shoes, coats and bags are ready.

This looks simple, but consider the following: have these rules been talked through with everyone, and has everyone agreed to them? Does the routine change depending on the day of the week or the mood of the household? The potential list of questions is endless, but what I am trying to say is that without clarity about a situation there is always potential for misunderstanding. A child is not necessarily being defiant if he just doesn't understand the script.

The key to changing a situation so that you see more of the behaviours you want to see is to provide opportunities for your child to receive lots of praise and encouragement for doing the right things. So, if getting out of bed in the morning is traditionally a tricky time, then think about how you can make this time run more smoothly. Perhaps a lot of preparation the night before might ease the tension.

Giving your children opportunities to get things right and to feel good about themselves is an excellent way of breaking the negative pattern of defiance. For many children this behaviour has become a habit that they have got into and sometimes only intervention from the parents can break the cycle.

If you think your child is being defiant simply because he needs or likes to feel in control, give him small areas of responsibility, and each time he completes his tasks without being asked, give him lots of praise. Involve him in drawing up a schedule of how to do things at crucial points in the day. It always surprises me how involving children in the planning can make even the most frantic times run smoothly. The key is to ensure that every person knows that they have a contribution to make and that if they carry this out the household will run more smoothly. Remember that children love to feel that they have fulfilled their part of any bargain and they will be pleased if you comment on how much you value their contribution.

The importance of praise

As we know, all children love to have their parents' notice when they have done something well. However, our fast pace of life can mean we only notice the things we have to correct. So remember to always praise the good behaviour you see and you will find you get more of it.

Match the method to the child

If you are struggling with a defiant child, there are a few things you can do to encourage her to be more compliant; however, the approach you take should be tailored to the age and personality of your child.

With very young children, up to the age of three years, stickers and star charts are good ways of reinforcing and reminding both your child and yourself that she has achieved what you want her to. As well as being rewarded with a sticker (which should lead to some sort of reward, for example, five stickers equal playing a game together, a trip to the shop, and so on), these successes should be talked about and praised.

If there are specific times of day when your child seems to be particularly defiant, such as at bedtime or mealtimes, then pay attention to her and her behaviour at this time and give stickers or prompts accordingly.

Time out is the most straightforward way of dealing with defiant children, and this is an area where the child's age is particularly relevant to how you enforce the discipline. Give your child fair warning and clearly let her know that her defiant behaviour will result in her being placed in time out: I have found that this is particularly helpful with young children up until the age of about ten.

If the behaviour does not stop, either place the child in (or ask older children from the age of six to go to) a fairly unstimulating room for a minute for each year of her life. Regardless of her age, all children five years and over should remain in time out for just five minutes.

When the allotted minutes are up, repeat your initial request to your child and praise her if she now does as you have asked. However, if she refuses to do as you ask again, repeat the time out sequence for the same amount of time.

This is an exhausting process at first, but eventually it does pay off. Be ready to be tested. I have had parents tell me that this method does not work with their children; but often this is because they have not been forceful or committed enough in their request – or they have given in because it has just seemed too hard to enforce.

For children with strong personalities a more measured way of tackling their behaviour is required. I am not saying that parents need to back off – more that they need to study their child carefully and note what they think they need to do in order to help her develop. As I've said earlier, some children find it important to feel in control and this is particularly true of children with very strong personalities. A child who is wilful will want to force her view and may try to argue her way out of a situation, so try to avoid these occasions by being very clear about what you expect from her and set up time limits within which the job you are asking her to do must be completed. This will give your child guidelines within which to work and will help her to have some sense of control. If you ask her to do something straight away the chances are you will only meet with a head-on confrontation.

A child who has little tolerance of her frustration will also need to be given jobs that are easily achievable. Be careful not to give strings of commands; in my experience children who find it difficult to tolerate frustration will only take or hear two to three instructions, so you'll be fighting a losing battle if you say things like, 'I want you to go upstairs, run the bath, get in, wash your hair and brush your teeth!' Stick to two linked instructions and show your child how pleased you are if she manages to do them.

Look to yourself

Again, as with many other difficult forms of your child's be-haviour, your key aim as a parent is to make sure that you model the behaviours you would like to see in your child. Be sure to notice your own behaviour and gradually fine-tune any rough edges in yourself.

Take care, too, when other adults or your child ask you to help out or to do something. Look at how you usually respond: if you answer negatively on many occasions then don't be surprised if your child does the same. By refusing to oblige you are giving your child the message that you are not flexible or helpful and this can sometimes become a rut that you and he can get stuck in, where the situation has become so difficult between you that you mirror each other's behaviour. As the adult it is your job to demonstrate to your child compliance and a willingness to be helpful and accommodating.

Similarly, if you find that you are always correcting your child's behaviour and limiting his decision-making and opportunities to take risks then you may be moulding a person who really struggles to feel in control and who then exerts this control by thwarting you when you ask for help.

Sometimes children might actually offer to do things but their parents say no because they want them to do something else. If you have a defiant child you need to capitalize on these moments and give him the opportunity to suggest ways in which he thinks he can be helpful. Learn to let go and put up with jobs not being completed quite as you would like them to be; the fact that your child is helping is a more important starting point.

One of the most effective parenting strategies is to be consistent. When trying to establish consistency try to spot areas where you slip up. How many times do you notice yourself asking your child to do something, getting a negative response

from him and then saying that you will do it yourself? This scenario becomes more complicated when your child then agrees to do the task and you say, 'It's too late now, I'm going to do it.' Sound familiar?

It doesn't take a genius to see how easily this can become a routine scenario between you and your child. Eventually he will begin to realize that if he holds out long enough he won't actually have to do anything, and that if he goes further and leaves agreeing to do it until the last minute it's even less likely that he will be expected to do anything.

This response also communicates something quite powerful about you as an adult. It might be a relief just to do something yourself, but by doing so you are suggesting that you can do things better than anyone else. The emotions that you are hiding (feeling very let down, upset and annoyed) will inevitably spill out into other areas of your life.

So don't just give up; take the time to try and negotiate with your child. Talk to him about why you ask him to help with jobs around the house, tell him about the massive contribution it makes to all of your lives if everyone does their share. You may also want to be quite honest and upfront and admit that not every job is going to be enjoyable but that every person who gets involved is a real help.

By keeping this dialogue going you will be helping yourself and your child to move forward together, rather than papering over the cracks of a relationship that doesn't acknowledge the difficulties you are having.

Give clear instructions

The way in which you give an instruction to a child is very important. Children, as with adults, need to know what is expected of them. Fuzzy instructions leave lots of room for defiance. For example, if I said, 'I want you to tidy your room today,' you would be quite right in thinking that you had all day to tidy up before I came to look. And certainly, the older your child, the longer the day would be! This statement is open to interpretation, so say what you want to happen and be explicit about how long she has to tidy her room.

How long to resolve?

This is a tricky question – how long is a piece of string? I think dealing with defiance is one of those lifelong learning experiences where you are constantly working out how much you give, who to and how often. (I say this because even as an adult there can be situations where others take advantage of your good nature and your willingness to be helpful.)

Essentially the situation is going to be changeable and it is up to you to recognize this. Notice the positive efforts that your child is making and see these as real signs of change for the better.

Remember, everyone falls backwards every so often, but it does not mean that all is lost.

Going forward

Helping your child to be compliant rather than defiant is key to her overall development and, ultimately, to the way that she will maintain and develop the relationships that she forms. All children need to see that by being compliant with their parent's wishes, and by doing what they are asked to do, they will help create a more harmonious atmosphere at home.

Tackling defiance by being stern and rigid really does not work: many children will just dig in their heels and the standoff between you and your child will begin. Similarly, pleading with her or trying to persuade her to do what you ask does not work either, as this can give her the impression that she has the upper hand and that you are at her beck and call – and that she can call the shots if she chooses to.

So instead, be fair in what you ask of your child. As a parent you want to have a household where everyone has their own unique role and where it is clear that everyone joins in to help the home run smoothly. Talking about the expectations that you have will allow everyone to say what they think they can contribute, and if the situation feels unequal you can draw attention to this fact.

Listen to your child and encourage her to talk about how she feels when she is asked to do jobs. Maybe you have a child who would prefer to have a predictable routine, which changes every so often, rather than living in a system where the jobs they are asked to do change daily. It sounds a bit military, but for some children this level of consistency and predictability might be the key to unlocking their compliance, because it means they will not be caught unawares.

Discuss the jobs that you would like some help with around the home and then ask your child to choose something that she thinks she could do regularly. Then, together, decide how frequently these jobs should be rotated amongst the other members of the family.

In addition to organizing what each child should do in the home, talk to your child and see whether together you can spot when you think the difficult times of the day are, for example, getting up in the morning, doing homework, and so on. Then discuss how you can tackle these areas: perhaps it would be helpful if homework or jobs around the house are completed before she settles down to relax in front of the television or play on the computer.

Use everyday routines as times to put incentives in place. For example, getting dressed and ready by a certain time will result in time to watch the television, and so on. Plan all these strategies together with your child so that she feels she has joint ownership of and responsibility for any of the decisions that you make.

Don't forget

○ Don't tackle defiance head-on with more defiance and anger – you'll only create a standoff.

○ Praise and reward any attempts by your child to do what you ask and get your friends and family to do the same if they see your children responding to your requests.

○ Involve your child in the planning of jobs so that he feels part of the process, and hopefully more inclined to help.

○ Try not to fall into situations where your child's defiant behaviour (for example, a tantrum or shouting) throws you off track and the job remains undone.

○ Try not to turn the situation into one where you are in sole control. Allow your children time to complete the job (within reasonable limits).

○ Make sure that you have consequences in place to deal with defiant behaviour that your child understands, for example, loss of time on a game, and so on.

○ Join in and name the jobs that you have to do so that children feel everyone has a part to play in making sure the household runs smoothly.

The road to a more enjoyable family life

Family life is full of highs and lows, but hopefully for most of us the highs will outweigh the lows. In my work I find that it helps to keep perspective on an issue if I acknowledge the good bits as well as the more difficult bits.

We seem to live in a society where we only discuss the negative features of being a parent rather than celebrating the more positive aspects. Stories about the bad or anti-social behaviour of children are frequently reported in the news and it is often the parents who are found to be at fault or lacking in some way. This can make parenting seem intolerably difficult and can also make the slightest behavioural issues we experience with our children feel like the end of the world. Everybody has an opinion on what a good parent is and how children should behave, so it can be tricky to believe that each phase will pass if handled by you in an appropriate way.

The behaviours that have been highlighted in the book are just a few of those you will encounter throughout your parenting years. Of course, there might well be many other areas that you will come up against, which may be unique to you and your child. However, many of the common behaviours your child will throw at you can be tackled with the help of some of the basic principles for thinking about and addressing each area.

I hope that, having got this far in the book, you have begun to think differently and have been keeping in mind some of the ideas which will help you address a range of behavioural problems in a strong and supportive way, including:

- Reflecting on your own behaviour.
- Thinking about the influence you have on your children.
- Considering the modelling you need to do to help your child develop.
- Thinking about the reasoning that is behind your child's behaviour.

Be realistic

Remember that the key to pacing yourself and not expecting difficult situations to be resolved overnight is being fluid in your role as parent. I have worked with families over a number of months and years where we have felt that we have crossed one hurdle only to find that the same issue comes up again and again – sometimes it reappears less pronounced than the last time, but not always.

However, these instances should be viewed not as a set-back, but as a reminder to us all that some behaviours can quickly take hold and become such entrenched patterns that you have to work incredibly hard to stop them taking over. The end result can only be achieved if all family members are committed to helping to find and contributing to a solution.

Each day brings very different behaviours, feelings and responses in all of us: you won't get it right all of the time – and to be honest you won't always have the energy to keep going with the strategies – but rather than say that the strategies are not working, be honest and admit that you have had a blip.

Stick with it!

Sometimes parents say the strategies we have planned together do not work: I know they work, but they take time and require parents to be able to be the 'bad guy' and to have faith in these methods. I believe that the long-term benefits outweigh the short-term pain. Being able to stand back from the situation and not take things personally is also, perhaps, the best way to survive what feels like a few rounds in the ring with your child when he is struggling to manage his behaviour.

Learn from your mistakes

Parents need to learn from their mistakes in the same way that we expect our children to. How many times have you heard yourself, or others, say to a child, 'and next time I don't expect you to make the same mistake'?

Parents need to absorb this message themselves: the fact that we find it difficult to change our behaviour at these crucial learning points shows us why it can be so difficult for our children to do the same. So for this reason, when our children find themselves in situations where they are told they need to learn and make the necessary changes, the adults must do the same. A stuck adult can hinder a child from making progress; the message you are giving her is that you are right and she is wrong.

If you are able to admit to your mistakes, remember that learning comes in very different forms and that you can't be expected to get things right all of the time. Be confident that your family has the capacity to change and not get tied into patterns and routines of problematic behaviour.

Allow your child to develop

It is important to remember, too, that children are destined to go through a number of developmental stages and this is perfectly normal. All parents should expect their children to have tantrums; they are part and parcel of developing independence and control. The need to master these skills occurs repeatedly. Other skills, such as language development, developing empathy and maintaining relationships are the things that children are trying to learn through their often testy behaviour. A child has to find his own path in order to work out how he will become his own person.

Such behaviours will take a child through a learning curve, and along the way he will explore:

- Independence.
- Developing social skills.
- Learning about control.
- Management of aggression, frustration and anger.
- Use of language.
- Relationships.
- Communication styles.
- Developing confidence.

If you think about your child's behaviour as your opportunity to help him to learn, the job can feel less frustrating. However, if you see your child's behaviour simply as his way of getting at you, it can be very difficult to shift your position and can even be quite destructive for your relationship with him. Essentially, the relationship that you have with your child has to be based on trust and the knowledge that each testing stage of his development can be survived because of the loving bond that you have.

If this is not a feeling that you have, and if there is a poor attachment between you, your child's behaviour can feel like a personal attack. However, take a step back and allow yourself a different view. This can be difficult when there are emotions involved, but what new and difficult situation will not call on your emotional resources?

Remind yourself that most often the behaviour is not personal – your child is merely trying to learn skills that are vital ingredients to helping him develop as a person. Once he has mastered these, and as he learns each one, it is the job of a parent to nurture and help maintain this good behaviour by providing opportunities to practise it in a range of situations. Then you will receive the pay-off for the work that you have done to help him through this bad time.

Try to focus on the aspects of your relationship with your child that give you hope. When you are in a difficult phase it can be hard to think back to the times when things were easier. Make time to remind yourself and your child of a different period in your lives; sit and look at old photos together and tell him how you felt, how proud you were and how much love you have for him. Ask him what he really enjoys doing with you and then set aside some time to do this. Even little activities – such as going shopping and taking a photo booth picture of the two of you to put on the fridge – can serve as a reminder of happy times and make you feel that it is worth all the effort to try even harder.

The bottom line is that parents don't have the option of giving up, and your child doesn't want you to – in spite of how difficult he is being. So remember that having the ability to forgive and work with your child and to offer him love is key to making sure you provide the secure emotional base that he needs to return to. I see this again and again with the parents I work with, and the one thing that their children are relying on is that their parents will still love them and remain optimistic that things will improve in the future.

Don't expect too much

Being realistic about what is ahead of you can help you to see the current situation in a more positive way. I also believe that having too high expectations of yourself and your own ability to cope with all the things that are thrown at you can cause its own problems.

The expectations of those around you can also put huge pressure on you, even if they are intended to be support-ive. Everybody – your parents, your friends and other family

Do your homework!

As with any job, especially one that you have never done before, it is reasonable to expect that you will need to do some research around the subject. Mix with other parents in order to learn some of the strategies that have been, and still are, helpful to them in managing their children's behaviour.

members – will all have views on how they think you are coping with your child. Keeping your self-confidence high when all around you expect you to fall is a difficult task, but if you formulate a rough view of how you hope to look after your child, then this will form a template for you to work from and enable you to absorb the help and support that is right for you.

It's a delicate balance, so don't become too rigid; accept help and advice if you think you need to, but you must also be sure to follow your own instincts.

In my view, parents put far too much pressure on themselves to get things right from the very beginning. Again, in a work situation it would be unheard of to think that you would immediately know what to expect and how to react when a situation arises. Some aspects of parenting are instinctive, but others are not and so need to be learnt. Don't pile the pressure on yourself just because you see others doing things differently: remember that the relationship you have with your child is unique to you, so therefore it is, naturally, different.

If you find yourself frequently getting into a state and starting to believe a situation is spiralling out of your control, try to plan things in your mind. Don't make the plans so complicated or rigid that there is no room for a situation to evolve naturally – pace yourself and don't give yourself unnecessary stress. I have always found it helpful to have loose plans that can be changed at the last minute; I can't say that it always happens, but it does make life more manageable. No parent can predict one day to the next, so allowing yourself freedom to change your mind is vital. Focus on doing what needs to be done; achieving any of the other things on your list is a bonus.

Having someone to talk to about the children every evening is also a good way to help you gain some perspective on how each day has been. I have always valued this opportunity, and I realized how vital it is when I returned to work and someone else looked after my children. I liked to get a 'debriefing' every night where the person looking after them told me about what the children had done that day. This chat kept me up to date with what my children were doing and allowed the carer to evaluate the day and to think about what had gone well and what still needed to be tackled the next day.

Keep a positive attitude

Remaining upbeat and positive when you have a screaming toddler or a stroppy pre-teen is, let's be honest, challenging. When you are caught in those moments it can feel easier to join in and have a tantrum yourself but, of course, as the reasonable adult it is important that you don't.

Each situation and outcome is governed quite heavily by the sort of person that you are. Thinking about your own characteristics is helpful, as it will guide your reactions. Consider whether you are someone who likes to feel in control, then ask yourself how much this contributes to the way you respond to different issues. Lots of parents and children suffer from being in situations where there are power struggles to establish who is in control; if this is your situation, step back and ask yourself whether it is really worth the pain. Is there a better way?

● Being in control is not about stifling a child's individuality; you want to let your children know that you are a safe pair of hands.

● Your children will trust you if you explain to them why you act in the way you do, for example, when using approaches such as time out you should tell your child why you are doing this, which should help her understand why she needs to change her behaviour.

● Try to keep an eye on how many of your interactions with your child offer warmth and support and how many are harsh. If the latter is more evident then you need to change your approach: an employer who only pointed out the things you did wrong would not be a great person to work for!

● Admit to your child that sometimes you have made the wrong call; at least this does not leave her feeling lost when things are inconsistent.

It's not all about control...

One of the many valuable lessons I have learned as a parent is that I cannot 'control' my children, and that this really isn't the relationship I want with them anyway. However, having said that, I can see why parents want to manage their children in this way as it can seem like the easier option.

Positivity comes from the type of person that you are. I have met parents who can be upbeat about the most difficult situations, and this in part seems to be due to their consistent strategy towards behaviour and their ability to see the long-term picture and also to remember that most phases pass with time. Keeping this long-term view in mind is very helpful as it can add perspective to a picture that can feel overly gloomy. It is also important to keep in mind the fact that you are facing ordinary behaviours that are part of regular development, despite how extraordinary these situations can feel.

If you have the type of personality that tends to find it difficult to be upbeat, then recognizing this in yourself will help you to consider your responses and change them to be more accommodating. A positive disposition can make difficult situations seem much more manageable. Maintaining this atmosphere in your house takes patience and perseverance, but by remaining upbeat you will help your child to develop a way of looking at the world. (The phrase glass half-full comes to mind, and this is certainly a metaphor that can help you to reach happier times.)

One way to maintain a positive frame of mind is to highlight the things that you notice about your child's behaviour that are good. If you feel that you have had a good morning, comment on this so that she hears your appreciation.

A fundamental part of the jigsaw that is often missing is congratulating yourself; this can help a child to realize that everyone needs some positive stroking. I have noticed that when I praise myself in front of my own children they are more likely to say positive things about themselves, and about me.

Use every opportunity to talk to your child in this way: when collecting her from school listen as she recalls her day and pick out the bits she says she enjoyed and expand on these. Give her the idea that there is always something positive to be taken from the day.

Be positive!

The parallels between adults and children and what we all need are everywhere. After a day at work it can be very damaging to your emotional state just to focus on the negative aspects: tomorrow is another day, so celebrate your achievements and see what impact it has on your next day.

Listen to your child

Making time to listen properly to your child is vital; not only does it give you an opportunity to really get to know him, but also it provides an opportunity for him to learn some fundamental rules about communication.

Think about how you and your family communicate: this includes how you talk with each other as well as how you listen to each other. There are often very different styles that each individual uses when communicating – there are those individuals who are more forceful when putting their point of view across, and others who are less so. Spend some time concentrating on this and think about the impact that each person in the family has on others. You may find that if you respond in a slightly different way, subtle differences will occur.

Ask yourself the following questions: who gets most of your attention, and how do they achieve this? If you find that you have fallen into a trap of responding to the loudest voice, think about what this communicates to one of your quieter children. Or it may be that you only have one child who finds it difficult to find his voice in a household where the adults take up a lot of the air space.

Family life gives us as parents a range of situations where we can pay attention to the issue of communication. At mealtimes, when everyone is sitting together, try to make sure that everybody has the opportunity to speak and insist that each person is listened to. Set the scene so that you and your family can get the maximum benefit. Try to eat together as many times a week as possible, make sure that background noise such as the television or the radio is switched off and insist that eating is the priority so no toys should be present. Most of all, encourage everyone to contribute and don't answer the telephone!

Sitting at the table makes for a more formal coming together, so plan other times when you are all sitting in the same room talking more generally, or play games where you can initiate a variety of conversations that include everyone. You will notice almost immediately how everyone listens to each other and values the time that you are spending together.

Make time to listen

Monitor your own individual responses to ensure that you give communication its rightful place. Are you someone who gives time to, and places high value on, what your child is saying? Or does her conversation become part of the general conversations in your house that do not really get listened to?

You know what I mean: how often do you find yourself involved in conversations where you are half listening and really have not got a clue what is being talked about, simply because you are preoccupied by so many other things? The impact on the child speaking can be devastating, as she knows she is being ignored and this is not good for her self-confidence.

These situations will allow children to think about how they speak out and listen to others in different situations, both in and out of the house. What you want is for your child to feel loved, appreciated and thought about. As adults, we like and want to be listened to and for our thoughts and opinions to be considered; the same rules apply to our children.

Be consistent

It's fairly obvious that having consistency is a good thing: being consistent ensures that you provide a base for your child that is predictable and reliable.

We all benefit from routines that provide us with structure. You might feel that you are consistent, but this is one of the hardest areas to police and a prime example of where stepping back or taking on board other people's opinions can really help. Situations vary, as do moods and temperaments, so what felt right as a reward or consequence one day may not feel right the next. Herein lies the difficulty: if a child is faced with a range of treats then she might find that easy to manage, but a range of consequences will not sit so easily with her.

I probably don't need to labour this point, but there are rules that we all need to follow. Establish your own consistent rules about what will happen if children behave well or if they are difficult. Try to keep to the rules that you make, but if you do stray, talk about why you both think that this happened then return as quickly as possible to what has been agreed.

Expectations also need to be consistent. If you expect your child to tidy away her toys then you should insist on this each day. By changing this rule you put the seed of doubt into her mind and it will become impossible for her to second guess what you are expecting her to do on any given day. If you find yourself getting into trouble with this, think about whether you have too many rules. On average, two or three are about the maximum most children can keep in mind at any one time.

Consistency between parents is also an area for attention. Couples have to make sure that they do not allow themselves to be divided. Setting up a good-cop, bad-cop system will only lead to more problems and make it difficult to present a united front. If children see this then they will, of course, capitalize on it. You both need to send out the message that you support each other, and if your opinion does differ over something, make sure these disagreements are discussed away from your child.

Engaging with your child

I have spent countless hours with parents who tell me that they spend time with their child; they are not lying, but it is the quality of the time spent together that I would question. Individual time with each of our children is very special, so spending time engaging with your child is about coming together with no distractions and making your time available to him exclusively. It is not going shopping or making dinner – these are all activities that can dilute the experience for him.

If you are truly going to spend time with your child then you need to be fairly disciplined. Make time to sit down without any interruptions and allow him to choose whatever he would like to do with you. A good part of the day to start practising this is often bedtime when, after a story, you can sit together and chat or play a quiet game.

Be proactive and look at where you can fit in this special time. Think about a typical day: it's probably full of the ordinary activities that are essential for making sure that a day runs smoothly, but try to identify any spaces where you can have ten minutes together with your child doing something that he wants to do. Play Eye Spy in the car, sit and read a book together at home, spend time in the garden or at the park. Whatever you do, you are aiming to give your child your undivided attention.

To manage this you will need to cut yourself off from the dreaded outside influences such as mobile phones and background noise, and forget about the endless list of jobs that always need to be done. You need to be relaxed so that your child does not feel either that you are in a hurry or that you have other things to do.

Difficult, I hear you say, and I do agree, but if you are to have a positive effect on your child's growing self-confidence and general wellbeing then spending time with him is a vital component of this. Not only does spending this sort of time with your child raise his confidence levels, but it also provides you and him with a very secure footing for your own relationship because he realizes that you want to be with him and that you enjoy his company. Time spent together will build the bond between you, and allow it to develop and change as your child grows.

Create family times

Family life is meant to be enjoyable, and on the whole it usually is. Children grow up very quickly and parents often feel that they have missed out simply due to the general busyness of family life.

It is wonderful to hear parents talk about the parts of family life that remain sacred and which, in effect, hold them together. Rituals such as having breakfast together, eating as a family each evening, watching the same television programme or film together or even all going to the cinema can make such a difference to the atmosphere at home. These sorts of activities are vital because they hold you together as a unit and give you the opportunity to monitor the changes.

If you keep family time as a basic expectation other situations which are not always planned will follow, simply because you will have established a way of being together that you all feel comfortable with.

Try making a list of all the times you regularly have together as a family. Compare it with those of other family members and then ask each individual what they enjoy doing together – even the very youngest children can answer these questions and this gives you the basis for a list that you can all agree on and stick to.

The key aim of this has to be enjoyment: there is nothing worse than having everyone gathered together for something that either only the parents or only the children enjoy. There must be something to be gained for everyone. For you the pleasure might not come from the actual activity, but more the sheer enjoyment of seeing your children happy and relaxed in your company. That is a priceless situation, and I'm sure most of us would give a lot to have that sort of relationship with our children.

Don't forget

o Remember that family life is always going to be full of highs and lows.

o Take each stage as it comes but try to think ahead positively. Children will not stay stuck in this rut for ever and there will always be some movement.

o You will make mistakes; don't try to cover them up but talk about what has happened and learn from them. If your child sees you doing this she will understand that everyone can get things wrong from time to time.

o Be proud of your child's development and acknowledge her progress – you want her to notice that she has improved as well.

o Don't take bad behaviour personally. Remember to be available with love and reassurance in the knowledge that things will get better.

o Spend time with your children together or individually and make sure that there is time for the family to all be together too. This will help children feel that they have a secure base to return to even when the going gets tough. It will also serve as a reminder to you that all your thinking and hard work is worth it.

o Remain positive, and upbeat, in the knowledge that children will test you in their quest to learn more about themselves.

What about you?

No situation is perfect. I have always wondered what perfect family life would look like and have numerous questions when parents present their home life to me in this way. It makes me want to ask them what is not being talked about and what is really going on beneath the surface. I'm not saying that the picture that is painted needs to be gloomy in order for it to be more believable, but just that a picture that shows the ups and downs of life is a more realistic one and a more healthy one, as well as one that puts less pressure on a family. Chocolate-box, picture-postcard images of life should be left where they belong – in the imagination.

All parents feel overwhelmed from time to time, and some-times even at a loss, when faced with the difficult behaviour thrown at them by their child. It can leave them feeling upset, depressed and hopeless – and these are certainly legitimate emotions. However, if these feelings do not pass they need to be addressed in order that you can move forward.

Where do you find the answers?

Parents who come to see me about their children's behaviour want to have their questions answered. They want to know why their child is behaving in the way that he is; they want to know what they can do about it; and, most of all, they want to know if something that they have done has contributed to the situation they and their child find themselves in.

When a child behaves badly it can seem as if everyone wants to know why it is happening and who is to blame for it, and this can mean even more pressure and upset for the parents. The blame often lands neatly at the door of parents; parents can come under considerable attack for not getting things right. Unfortunately a child's behaviour problems are not like a bug or an infection – you can't see a doctor and pick up a prescription. The 'treatment' will take time, a lot of thought and energy to resolve.

I hope that you have gained something from reading this book and can now see that all children's difficulties are multi-layered, and that in order to find a solution to their behavioural issues each member of the family has to reflect on their own unique position and possible contribution to what is taking place. In addition, parents need to think about the message their child may be trying to convey – many children behave in certain ways because they have no other way of communicating their worries and problems.

In difficult times parents have to give some thought to, and take responsibility for, the bits of the problems that belong to them. The position you hold as a parent is significant: whatever you are experiencing will clearly have an impact on your child's behaviour, and you need to be aware of this if you want to prevent issues developing. Some children seem to have finely tuned antennae which are wired up to the emotional climate in a house, and their behaviour at any one time will tell you how things are for them.

Why now?

Parents need to develop a way of questioning what they think is happening in order to try to make sense of it for themselves first. The question 'why now?' is a good place to start because it gives you an opportunity to look around and think about why you are concerned about a particular behaviour at that time. It also allows you to reflect on why an issue that may have come up before is now having a quite different impact on you when before you could cope.

Being a parent is hard work, and it is a job made more complex by ordinary everyday life experiences which will affect your ability to manage situations – ignore these at your peril. I have sat with parents who come to me completely at a loss as to why their child is behaving in the way that he is. However, once we begin to talk we can uncover some of the parents' issues which are having an impact on their ability to respond to their child in a constructive way. Issues such as stress, anxiety, bereavement, illness, separation, relationship problems and pregnancy are just a few of the triggers that can lead to a change in the situation at home.

You may be feeling low and you may know why this is, or you really might not have a clue. Either way this feeling will affect your ability to see things clearly. In fact your child's difficulties may seem far worse than they actually are simply because you are struggling personally. Admitting to yourself that you are feeling down, especially if you have been feeling like this for a while, can seem daunting, and with the never-ending responsibility of looking after children there can seem to be no way you can stop and focus. But remember that looking after your own needs is paramount if you are to improve the situation for yourself and also for your child.

You may feel that everybody is judging you, and possibly unfairly. Some people might just think you are fed up, others that you are being moody and some might actually see the real problem for what it is. The impact of your emotional state on a child also varies: some children may adapt to your behaviour and just get on with life, while others will detect something is wrong but will only be able to express their worry through their behaviour.

How you notice the impact of your various emotions on yourself and the rest of the family is important. I am full of admiration for what some parents have to manage, but also disappointed that people around them do not notice what they are struggling with or that they are not receiving any support. Parents often struggle on with few support systems, and this can add to the strain, so don't be shy to ask for help.

The pressures that parents put on themselves to get things right can, and often do, lead to high levels of anxiety. Children are fantastic at noticing when their parents are stressed and they can respond to this by behaving in a more challenging way. Whether they are doing so or not, you will be in a heightened state of awareness and so your reactions will inevitably be different. I know this from sitting in family sessions where the children might become agitated and a parent responds

quite forcefully due to their own anxious state. If you do not notice that you are anxious then one of the likely outcomes will be that everyone will be living in a state of high alert worried about where the next outburst might come from.

Ongoing relationship problems between parents can be one of the most difficult things to spot as they may be denying the conflict. Parents often become involved in an elaborate dance where they avoid each other in order to stop the children from finding out what is actually going on. This can lead to parents exhibiting all sorts of strange behaviours, and placing unmanageable and unreasonable pressure on themselves.

If this is the case you need to call on your emotional resources and address the situation in the right way so as not to give children confusing messages about what adults do when they are not getting on. Putting a brave face on things impacts on everyone, not least the parents who are feeling very differently inside from what their outward expressions suggest.

As difficult as it may seem, parents need to find a way to talk about their behaviour and the breakdown of their relationship. They also need to find solutions that protect both the adults and the children, which might mean agreeing to try to mend the situation through counselling, or even by separating. Don't kid yourself that staying together for the sake of the children is the best option – this does not provide a helpful model of family life. Parents inevitably resent this situation and their children will grow up in a cool atmosphere with adults who cannot work together or think about them consistently.

Other more ordinary family events, such as having a baby, can cause a multitude of unexpected feelings. You may be unsure of how your ongoing relationships with other children will be, or whether or not you will be able to cope.

The list of such influential events is endless, and the feelings that go with those – both major and minor – can stir people up to the extent that they feel that they are not themselves. The unpredictable nature of life means that both the positive and negative feelings which accompany certain situations can lead to surprising outcomes. Take care of yourself, or else you run the risk of falling into a downward spiral where things can look very difficult and you could find it very hard to remain upbeat.

Don't let setbacks get you down

Noticing that you have hit a setback is one thing, doing something about it is another. Taking care of yourself can come as a bit of an afterthought. Parents can become so absorbed in the job of parenting that they forget to look after themselves. The bottom line is that if you do not look after your own needs it will be even harder to focus on those of your child.

So start to think about yourself.

● Recognize that setbacks are often temporary: how you feel today may not be how you feel tomorrow. Watch your reactions carefully. If you can pick yourself up after a few days, fine, but if not it might be time to try another strategy.

● Talk to you partner about how you are feeling. Use this as an opportunity to see what they have noticed and to decide which issue needs to be tackled first. You may have to take a step back and allow your partner to take the lead here.

● Give yourself some time off. Try to be disciplined about this or it won't happen. Ask family and friends to look after your child, even if it's just for an hour. This will give you time to rest, go out or just have some time for yourself. Accept that you might not get much done, but you should be able to recharge a little and be able to gain some perspective on your situation. Your child won't suffer just because you have an hour away.

● Talk to family and friends, but pick those people carefully: you want to be able to talk to people who listen and who will not be judgemental. Discussing things in this way will help you explore how best to tackle the issues you are facing. You may come away feeling better and so more able to move on, or you may come away thinking you need to have more time and space to help you cope better.

● Think back to the time before you had children. Try to identify some of the activities you did which helped keep you happy and healthy. Perhaps you took exercise, went out with friends or took a day trip. You might feel it's impossible to do these things now, but with determination you can find a way. Perhaps you could exercise with your child in the buggy, or ask friends to come over one evening and each bring some food or order a take-away so you don't have to cook, or take a trip somewhere that makes you feel that you are away from it all.

○ Time out away from home may just be too problematic, so instead try to separate yourself from your child while at home. Doing this every now and again is vital to make you feel that you are still sane. Slow the pace of life down by taking yourself off to a separate room and visualizing a favourite place, and while doing so, close your eyes and regulate your breathing. Do this whenever you feel yourself becoming stressed. Or just give yourself your own 'time out'. Remember, it should not be for longer than five minutes and should only be done when your child is in a safe place, but it is an excellent protective strategy for you when you feel that everything is getting too much and you think the situation may get out of hand. Stepping back like this to calm down gives you a brief moment to get your head back together and prepare yourself for whatever is ahead.

Don't struggle alone

Depending on the issue, you may want to talk to your GP and get some help. Many surgeries now have an impressive range of services that offer short-term opportunities to meet with a professional to talk about what is on your mind. Don't underestimate the powerful effect of talking to someone who is outside of your family or circle of friends. It can feel a bit exposing, so remember to take things at your own pace and give yourself space after each session to relax and do things that are not demanding.

Some parents realize that having children stirs up feelings and issues that cannot be resolved in the short term. This may include issues such as difficulties in your relationships, feelings of unhappiness and depression, or simply how overwhelmed you are feeling by your situation or the responsibility of parenthood. These sorts of issues might need to be attended to in a far more systematic way and may involve long-term treatment by professionals, such as therapists. GPs can often advise you of the ways to access help, or they will offer to refer you to your local community mental health service for more information and advice.

Parenting requires so much from us all as individuals that it is no wonder it is full of ups and downs. The lack of preparation for this job and the sheer emotional investment that is needed to undertake it undoubtedly takes its toll on even the most robust individuals. That said, being a parent may well be both the best and the most difficult experience that many of us will encounter. However, the joy you will get from seeing your child develop and the realization that you made a positive contribution to this development is, I believe, what drives many of us on. It is this happiness and satisfaction that keeps us believing we can nurture and love each of our children, so that as they move through each of the developmental stages we all survive and live to face the challenges of another day.

Resources

www.bbc.co.uk/parenting
The BBC website provides comprehensive advice and information, and links to further resources.

www.parentlineplus.org.uk
Freephone: 0808 800 2222

Available 24 hours a day, 7 days a week, ParentlinePlus is a free and confidential telephone helpline staffed by trained volunteers who offer information and support, and the chance for parents to talk to someone about the issues they are facing.

www.parentcentre.gov.uk
Tel: 0870 000 2288 (DfES HQ)

Provides helpful information for parents of children of all ages, while offering parent-to-parent and expert-to-parent support via the internet chat forums. It is part of the official Department for Education and Skills (DfES) website.

www.surestart.gov.uk
Tel: 0870 0002288

Sure Start is a government programme designed to help every child have the best start in life. The website gives information about early years education, childcare, health, tax credits and family support.

www.raisingkids.co.uk
A website for parents of children of all ages, providing expert parenting advice, parenting news and information, and suggestions for fun family activities.

www.oneparentfamilies.org.uk
Tel: 0800 018 5026

The website provides wide-ranging information for lone parents, including downloadable factsheets.

www.workingfamilies.org.uk

Working Families is the UK's leading work–life balance organization. Their website offers useful information for all working parents.

www.youngminds.org.uk

Tel: 0800 018 2138

National charity committed to improving the mental health of children and young people. They offer information and advice on mental health issues for young people and their families. There is a section on the website that specifically for parents: www.youngminds.org.uk/parents.